Grand Diplôme® Cooking Course

Volume 13

Grand Diplôme®
Cooking Course

A Danbury Press Book

The Danbury Press

a division of Grolier Enterprises, Inc.

Robert B. Clarke   Publisher

This book has been adapted from the Grand Diplôme Cooking Course, originally published by Purnell Cookery, U.S.A.

Purnell Grand Diplôme Editorial Board

Rosemary Hume and Muriel Downes
Principals, London Cordon Bleu Cookery
School, England

Anne Willan	Editor
Eleanor Noderer	Associate Editor
Sheryl Julian	Assistant Editor
John Paton	Managing Editor
José Northey	Co-ordinating Editor
Peter Leather	Art Editor
Charles F. Turgeon	Wine Consultant
Joy Langridge	Consultant Editor

Library of Congress Catalog Card Number: 72-13896
© Phoebus Publishing Company/BPC Publishing Limited, 1971/1972/1979
Filmsetting by Petty and Sons Ltd., Leeds, England.
Printed in the United States of America

4567899

All recipes have been tested either at the Cordon Bleu Cookery School in London or in our U.S. test kitchens.

Note: all recipe quantities in this book serve 4 people unless otherwise stated.

Contents

From the Editor

Aromatic cumin and coriander, scented fenugreek, fiery hot cayenne and many other spices combine in curry, the pungent mixture so evocative of the East. But you will soon discover in Volume 13 of your Grand Diplôme Cooking Course that curry is only half the story of the **Cooking of India and Pakistan.** For it is not only the subtle blend of spices, but also the many accompaniments that make an authentic curry memorable – choose from sweet and tart chutneys, smooth dahl (lentil purée), crisply fried breads, rice pilaus, hot pickles and cooling raitas, made with a curd of sour milk, similar to yogurt. Equally diverse are the fish, fowl, meat and vegetable salads in **Antipasto Appetizers**; when cleverly combined they make a meal in miniature before the main course.

From the second feature on **Variety Meats** you can sample such gourmet delights as brains Bourguignon, in a red wine sauce with mushrooms, and sweetbreads baked with prunes and garnished with chestnuts. Equally elegant are crêpes Suzette, flamed in style at the table, or lobster crêpes, filled with a luxurious combination of fresh lobster, mushrooms, brandy and cream. Both recipes are a part of the second feature on **Crêpes.**

The **Menus** in this Volume vary from a delicious dinner for four to a lavish cold buffet for 12 or a coffee party planned to serve as few or as many guests as you care to invite. Any **Leftovers** will take on a new look in dishes like cold ham soufflé, and kromeskis – pieces of shrimp, chicken or veal, wrapped in bacon, dipped in batter and deep fried.

Buttery brioches, flaky Danish pastries, fresh doughnuts and other **Rich Yeast Breads and Coffeecakes** is another culinary art made easy by following the methods of the Cordon Bleu Cookery School in London. You will quickly progress from basic coffeecake dough to creations like an Easter ring, topped with soft icing and decorated with walnuts, candied cherries and angelica. Homemade **Candies** are also certain of success, whether it be melting fondant flavored with lemon or crunchy walnut brittle, golden with crisp caramel. Happy cooking and Bon Appétit!

Anne Willan

Give the perfect coffee party with a colorful spread of sandwiches ranging from crab with cucumber to salami with green pepper. If you choose just a few, remember to contrast as many flavors, colors and textures as possible, and always cut party sandwiches into sizes that are easy to handle. For those with a sweet tooth there is a wide selection of simple cakes and cookies, like date bread studded with pitted dates and walnut cookies sandwiched with honey.

THE PERFECT COFFEE PARTY

Assorted Sandwiches

Quick Coffeecake

Date Bread   Apricot Nut Bars

Sand Tarts   Priory Cookies

English Flapjacks   Coffee Buns

Coffee Butterfly Cakes

Hazelnut or Walnut Cookies

COFFEE PARTY SANDWICHES

Choose a selection of thin crisp wafers or crackers and very thinly sliced white and dark rye breads. Each of the following toppings and fillings is enough for 6–8 open sandwiches or 16–20 finger sandwiches. Arrange the sandwiches on large platters or trays and keep in a cool place covered with plastic wrap until ready to serve.

OPEN SANDWICHES

Roquefort Topping

$\frac{1}{4}$ lb Roquefort cheese
1 small package (3 oz) cream cheese
2–3 tablespoons sherry
6–8 crisp wafers

Method
Mash the cheeses together with a fork until they are as smooth as possible. Gradually work in enough sherry to make a very soft mixture; spread this on crisp wafers.

Cheese and Pickle Topping

6–8 thin slices of Gruyère or Gouda cheese
2 tablespoons finely chopped sweet cucumber pickles
$\frac{1}{4}$ cup butter, softened
black pepper, freshly ground
6–8 crisp wafers or crackers

Method
Combine the butter with pickles and season with pepper. Spread the topping on crisp wafers or crackers and cover with thin slices of cheese.

Cheddar Cheese and Pimiento Topping

1 cup grated Cheddar cheese
2 slices of canned pimiento, drained and chopped
3–4 tablespoons mayonnaise
6–8 crisp wafers or crackers
2 slices of bacon, fried until crisp and drained

Method
Mix the cheese with pimiento and add enough mayonnaise to bind the mixture. Spread on the crackers or wafers. Crumble the bacon and sprinkle on top of each.

Curried Cheese Topping

1 small package (3 oz) cream cheese
$\frac{1}{2}$–1 teaspoon curry powder
8 ripe olives, pitted and chopped
1 teaspoon chopped chives
6–8 crisp wafers

Method
Blend cream cheese, curry powder to taste, olives and chives together. Spread on crisp wafers.

Cheese and Anchovy Topping

1 small package (3 oz) cream cheese
1 tablespoon anchovy paste (or to taste)
$1\frac{1}{2}$ tablespoons butter, softened
$\frac{1}{2}$ teaspoon Worcestershire sauce
6–8 crisp wafers

Method
In a bowl work the cheese, butter, anchovy paste and Worcestershire sauce together. Spread on the crisp wafers.

Ham and Cream Cheese Topping

4 thin slices of lean cooked ham
1 small package (3 oz) cream cheese
2 tablespoons butter, softened
1 tablespoon finely chopped chutney
1 tablespoon chopped parsley
6–8 crisp wafers

Method
Cut the ham in thin julienne strips. Work the cream cheese, butter, chutney and parsley together and spread on thin crisp wafers. Sprinkle the top generously with thin strips of ham.

Herring and Cream Cheese Topping

1–2 herring pieces in wine sauce
1 small package (3 oz) cream cheese
3 tablespoons butter, softened
6–8 crisp wafers
black pepper, freshly ground

Herring pieces in wine sauce are available by the pound at delicatessens or in 8 oz jars at most supermarkets.

Method
Work cream cheese and butter together until creamy. Spread on crisp wafers. Pat fish with paper towels to remove excess sauce; cut into thin strips discarding any bones. Lay in a lattice on cheese; sprinkle a little black pepper on top.

Sardine Topping

1 can sardines in olive oil,
   drained
1 tablespoon lemon juice
½ teaspoon dry mustard
black pepper, freshly ground
few drops of Tabasco
3–4 tablespoons mayonnaise
6–8 crisp wafers
few sprigs of watercress
   (optional)

Method

Mash the sardines with a fork
and stir in lemon juice,
mustard, black pepper, Tabasco and enough mayonnaise
to bind the mixture. Spread
on crisp wafers and garnish
with sprigs of watercress, if
you like.

Shrimp Topping

¼ lb cooked, peeled shrimps,
   coarsely chopped
3 tablespoons butter, softened
6–8 thin slices of wholewheat
   bread, crusts removed
3 tablespoons capers, drained
1 tablespoon lemon juice
3–4 tablespoons mayonnaise

Method

Spread butter on the slices of
bread. Combine the shrimps
with capers, lemon juice and
enough mayonnaise to bind
the mixture and spread on the
bread. Cut the slices into open
finger sandwiches.

FILLED SANDWICHES

Brown and White Rolled Sandwiches

3 thin slices of white bread,
   crusts removed
3 thin slices of dark rye or
   pumpernickel bread,
   crusts removed
3 tablespoons butter, softened
¼ lb liverwürst
½ cup pimiento-stuffed olives,
   chopped
3–4 tablespoons mayonnaise

Method

Spread the slices of bread
with the butter. Mash the
liverwürst with a fork and stir
in the chopped olives. Add
enough mayonnaise to bind
the mixture and spread on the
buttered bread. Roll each slice
like a jelly roll and cut in slices.

Salami Filling

¼ lb sliced salami
½ green pepper, cored, seeded
   and very finely chopped
2 scallions, very finely chopped
¼ cup ripe olives, pitted and
   chopped
3–4 tablespoons mayonnaise
24–30 slices of thin party rye
   bread

Method

Chop salami finely or work it
through a food mill. Combine
it with green pepper, scallions
and olives. Stir in enough
mayonnaise to bind the mixture and spread on 12–15
slices of party rye bread. Top
each with another slice of
bread.

Tongue Filling

3–4 slices of cooked tongue
3 tablespoons butter, softened
6–8 thin slices of rye bread
   with caraway seeds, crusts
   removed
2 teaspoons Dijon-style
   mustard
1 lettuce heart, shredded

Method

Spread butter on the slices of
bread. Spread a thin layer of
mustard on half the slices,
cover these with the shredded
lettuce and slices of tongue.
Top each with another slice of
bread and cut into squares or
strips.

Crab Filling

1 cup (8 oz) crab meat, flaked
juice of ½ lemon
3–4 tablespoons mayonnaise
8–10 thin slices of white
   bread, crusts removed
3 tablespoons butter, softened
1 cucumber, peeled and thinly
   sliced

Method

Mix the crab meat with the
lemon juice and add enough
mayonnaise to bind the mixture. Spread 4–5 slices of
bread with butter and top
with crab mixture. Cover each
with thin slices of cucumber
and another slice of bread.
Cut in quarters or into finger
sandwiches.

Mayonnaise

For 1 cup: in a bowl beat
2 egg yolks with ¼ tea-
spoon salt, and pinch each
of pepper and dry mustard
with a small whisk or
wooden spatula until thick.
Measure ¾ cup oil. Add 2
tablespoons of oil drop by
drop; the mixture will
then be very thick. Stir in
1 teaspoon wine vinegar.
Remaining oil can be
added more quickly (1
tablespoon at a time,
beaten thoroughly
between each addition
until smooth, or in a thin
steady stream if using a
blender). When all oil has
been added, add 1½ table-
spoons more wine vinegar
with more seasoning to
taste. To thin and lighten
mayonnaise, add a little
hot water. For a coating
consistency, thin with a
little cream or milk.

Watchpoint: mayonnaise
curdles very easily, so add
oil drop by drop at first,
then very slowly until
thick, when you can add
it in a slow steady stream.
If mayonnaise curdles,
start with a fresh yolk in
another bowl and work
well with seasonings.
Then add curdled mixture
drop by drop. Be sure all
ingredients are at room
temperature before start-
ing.

COFFEE PARTY CAKES AND COOKIES

Date Bread

$\frac{3}{4}$ cup pitted dates, quartered
$\frac{1}{4}$ cup butter
$1\frac{1}{3}$ cups dark brown sugar
$\frac{3}{4}$ cup water
1 egg, beaten well
2 cups flour
$\frac{1}{2}$ teaspoon salt
1 teaspoon baking soda

Medium loaf pan
($8\frac{1}{2}$ X $4\frac{1}{2}$ X $2\frac{1}{2}$ inches)

Method
Grease pan and set oven at moderate (350°F).

Melt the butter and brown sugar in the water over low heat; let cool, then pour into beaten egg. Sift flour, salt and baking soda together into a bowl; make a well in center. Pour in egg mixture, add dates, stir until smooth. Pour batter into prepared pan; bake in heated oven for about 50 minutes or until a toothpick inserted in center comes out clean. Turn out onto a wire rack to cool, and cut into thin slices to serve.

Apricot Nut Bars

1 cup coarsely chopped dried apricots
$\frac{3}{4}$ cup boiling water
$1\frac{1}{2}$ cups flour
$\frac{1}{2}$ teaspoon salt
$\frac{1}{2}$ cup shortening
$1\frac{1}{4}$ cups sugar
1 cup coarsely chopped pecans
2 eggs, beaten to mix
confectioners' sugar (for sprinkling)

13 X 9 inch cookie pan

Makes 24 bars.

Method
Pour the boiling water over the apricots and let stand 30 minutes.

Set oven at moderate (350°F) and grease the cookie pan.

Sift flour with salt. In a bowl rub the shortening into the flour with the fingertips. When the mixture resembles crumbs, stir in the sugar and pecans and make a well in the center. Add the eggs, apricots and water and stir in the flour to make a smooth batter. Spread in the prepared pan and bake in the heated oven for 30–35 minutes or until the mixture is brown and springs back when lightly pressed with a fingertip. Cool a little in the pan, then turn out on a wire rack to cool completely. Sprinkle with confectioners' sugar and cut into 3 X $1\frac{1}{2}$ inch bars.

Hazelnut or Walnut Cookies

1 cup hazelnuts, browned and ground, or $\frac{3}{4}$ cup chopped walnuts
$\frac{1}{2}$ cup butter
$\frac{1}{3}$ cup sugar
1 cup flour, sifted

For filling
$\frac{1}{4}$ cup thick honey, Damson plum jam, or apple butter
confectioners' sugar (for sprinkling)

$2\frac{1}{2}$ inch round cookie cutter

These cookies can be made 1–2 days before and stored, unfilled, in an airtight container. Makes 15 sandwiched cookies.

Method
Cream the butter until soft, gradually add sugar and beat until light and fluffy. Mix flour with nuts and work this mixture, half at a time, into the butter and sugar. When dough is smooth, wrap in wax paper and chill 15–20 minutes or until firm.

Set oven at moderate (350°F).

Roll out dough on a lightly floured board to about $\frac{1}{4}$ inch thickness. Cut out circles of dough with cookie cutter and prick the tops lightly with a fork. Place cookies on prepared baking sheet and bake in heated oven for 10–12 minutes or until beginning to brown around the edges. Take cookies from oven and cool slightly before removing from baking sheet and cooling on a wire rack.

When cookies are cold, sandwich together with honey or jam or apple butter. Sprinkle the tops with confectioners' sugar.

> ## To Brown Hazelnuts
> Spread the nuts on a baking sheet and bake in a moderately hot oven (375°F) for 8–10 minutes or until the brown skins begin to flake. Rub the nuts briskly in a rough cloth with the hands until the dark skins fall off.

English Flapjacks

2 cups rolled oats
6 tablespoons butter
$\frac{1}{2}$ cup granulated or dark brown sugar
2 tablespoons honey

8 inch square cake pan

These can be made 1–2 days before and stored in an airtight container. Makes 16.

Method
Grease cake pan; set oven at moderate (350°F).

Melt butter in a saucepan and blend in the sugar and honey. Mix in the rolled oats thoroughly.

Press mixture into prepared cake pan and bake in heated oven for about 25–30 minutes. Flapjacks will be soft when hot but will become firmer on cooling; cut them into squares while still warm.

Coffeecake with cinnamon topping, date bread, coffee buns and sponge cake (recipe is given in Volume 6) are good with coffee

Quick Coffeecake

1½ cups flour
pinch of salt
2 teaspoons baking powder
¼ cup shortening
¾ cup sugar
1 egg, beaten to mix
½ cup milk

*8 inch square cake pan or
large loaf pan
(9 X 5 X 3 inches)*

Method

Grease and lightly flour the pan; set oven at moderately hot (375°F).

Sift the flour, salt and baking powder together in a bowl. Rub in the shortening with the fingertips, stir in the sugar and make a well in the center.

Mix the beaten egg with milk and pour into well. Stir until a thick batter forms, then beat vigorously for 4—5 minutes to thicken it. Pour batter into prepared pan; cover with one of the suggested toppings.

Bake in heated oven for about 30 minutes or until a toothpick inserted in the center comes out clean. Cut coffeecake in wedges to serve; if using a square pan, cut in squares. It is best eaten warm.

Cinnamon Topping

2 teaspoons ground cinnamon
½ cup coarsely chopped
  walnuts
⅔ cup dark brown sugar

Method

Sprinkle walnuts over top of the unbaked coffeecake. Mix cinnamon and brown sugar together, sprinkle on top and bake.

Marmalade Topping

3 tablespoons marmalade
½ cup flour
⅔ cup brown sugar
2 tablespoons melted butter
1 tablespoon light cream

Method

Mix all the ingredients together and spread on top of the unbaked coffeecake and bake.

Pineapple Topping

1 can (8½ oz) crushed pineapple
¼ cup butter
¾ cup dark brown sugar

Method

Cream the butter, beat in the sugar until mixture is light and fluffy and stir in the crushed pineapple. Spread over unbaked coffeecake and bake.

Apple Topping

1 large tart apple, pared, cored
  and sliced
1½ teaspoons cinnamon
3 tablespoons sugar

Method

Press apple into surface of unbaked coffeecake. Combine cinnamon and sugar, sprinkle over the top and bake.

Candied Fruit and Nut Topping

½ cup apricot jam glaze
½ cup chopped walnuts
¼ cup chopped candied
  pineapple
¼ cup chopped red and green
  candied cherries

Method

Bake the coffeecake without

a topping, turn out and cool on a wire rack. Brush the top and sides thickly with apricot jam glaze and pour any remaining glaze on top. Mix the walnuts and candied fruits, spread them on top of the cake and press lightly so they stick to the glaze.

Sand Tarts

2 cups flour
½ teaspoon salt
1 teaspoon baking powder
½ cup butter
½ teaspoon vanilla
1 cup sugar
1 egg
1 egg yolk

For topping
little milk (for brushing)
3 tablespoons sugar
1 teaspoon cinnamon

Diamond-shaped cookie cutter

These tarts can be made 2—3 days before and stored in an airtight container. Makes about 36 tarts.

Method

Sift the flour, salt and baking powder together into a bowl. Cream butter with vanilla until soft, gradually add sugar and beat until light and fluffy. Add egg and egg yolk and mix thoroughly. Stir in sifted flour mixture, work dough until smooth, wrap in wax paper and refrigerate for several hours or overnight.

Set oven at moderate (350°F).

Divide dough into 2—3 portions and roll out 1 portion at a time as thinly as possible on a lightly sugared board. Cut out shapes from dough with cookie cutter and place these on a baking sheet. Brush tops with a little milk, then sprinkle with a little of the sugar mixed with the cinnamon and bake in heated oven for 8—10 minutes or until edges are a delicate brown. Turn onto a wire rack to cool.

Priory Cookies

1 cup flour
$\frac{1}{2}$ teaspoon baking powder
$\frac{1}{4}$ teaspoon salt
$\frac{1}{4}$ teaspoon cream of tartar
$\frac{1}{2}$ cup butter
$\frac{1}{2}$ cup sugar
$1\frac{1}{2}$ cups ($\frac{1}{4}$ lb) rolled oats
1 teaspoon baking soda
    dissolved in 2 teaspoons
    hot water
2 tablespoons honey, warmed

These cookies are named after the religious houses (priories) where they were made. They can be baked 2–3 days ahead and stored in an airtight container. Makes about 32 cookies.

Method

Sift the flour, baking powder, salt and cream of tartar together into a mixing bowl.

Cream butter in a bowl, gradually add sugar and beat until mixture is light and fluffy. Stir in rolled oats, the baking soda and water mixture, honey and the sifted flour mixture. Work until the dough is well mixed. Let stand 30 minutes.

Grease a baking sheet and set oven at moderate (350°F).

Place dough, a teaspoon at a time, on the prepared baking sheet, leaving space between each spoonful, and flatten dough with a wet fork. Bake in heated oven for about 8 minutes or until golden brown. Put the cookies on a wire rack to cool.

Another version of quick ▶
coffeecake has a topping of candied fruit and nuts

Coffee Buns

3 cups self-rising flour
pinch of salt
6 tablespoons shortening
$\frac{2}{3}$ cup dark brown sugar
1 egg
1 tablespoon dry instant
    coffee (to flavor)
about $\frac{1}{4}$ cup milk
1 cup quantity of coffee glacé
    icing (see Index) or
    coffee butter cream frosting
    (see page 52)

To be at their best, these buns must be made on the day they are served. Makes 14.

Method

Grease 2 baking sheets; set oven at hot (425°F).

Sift flour and salt together into a mixing bowl. Rub in shortening with the fingertips until the mixture resembles crumbs and mix in the sugar; make a well in the center.

Beat egg with instant coffee and add enough milk to make $\frac{1}{2}$ cup liquid. Add to the flour mixture and work until dough is well mixed.

Divide dough into 14 even-sized pieces; shape with hands into rounds or ovals. Place on prepared baking sheets and bake in heated oven for about 15 minutes or until lightly browned. Cool on a wire rack.

When cold, spread a little coffee glacé icing on top of buns or split each in half and fill with a little coffee butter cream frosting.

Coffee Butterfly Cakes

Cut a horizontal slice off top of coffee buns; spread a generous spoonful of coffee butter cream frosting on buns. Halve top slices; stick into frosting like butterfly wings.

Easter ring (recipe is on page 18)

YEAST BREADS AND COFFEECAKES

Plain bread is a staple in any household but sweet yeast breads are usually a luxury because they are enriched with expensive ingredients like butter, eggs, nuts and candied fruits.

These rich doughs have a soft crust and a spongy texture. They can be divided into three categories: coffeecakes, mixed by the same method as regular bread dough but with extra ingredients added; brioches, where yeast is added in a different way than for regular bread dough, and Danish pastries and croissants made with a yeast, flour and water dough that is rolled in layers with butter as for flaky puff pastry.

These doughs need more careful handling than regular breads. If you are inexperienced with using yeast, start with the simpler recipes like stollen, and be sure to read the detailed instructions for regular yeast breads in Volume 7.

COFFEECAKES

There are many kinds of coffeecakes and the basic dough for most is made the same way, although the proportions of ingredients may vary. The dough can be kneaded by hand or in an electric mixer with a dough hook.

Yeast is a living plant that needs warmth and moisture to grow. It thrives at a temperature around 80°F; excess cold will retard or check (but not kill) the growth; strong heat will kill it completely.

Both dry and compressed yeast are normally dissolved in lukewarm liquid – liquid at blood heat – that feels neither warm nor cool to the touch. For yeast to work in ideal conditions, it must be thoroughly distributed throughout the dough by kneading until mixture is smooth and elastic. Then it is left to rise in a warm, preferably damp, atmosphere at around 80°F.

Basic Dough for Coffeecakes

For 4 cup quantity
4 cups flour
$\frac{1}{2}$ teaspoon salt
1 cup milk
$\frac{1}{2}$ cup butter
1 package dry or 1 cake compressed yeast
$\frac{1}{2}$ cup sugar
2 eggs, beaten to mix

This recipe is given in Volume 9 but is repeated here for easy reference.

Method
Sift flour with salt into a warm bowl. Warm milk with butter until melted, then cool to lukewarm. Sprinkle or crumble yeast on top and leave 5 minutes or until dissolved. Stir in sugar and eggs.

Make a well in the flour, add yeast mixture and stir to form a smooth dough. Work with the hand until the dough pulls away from the sides of the bowl, then turn out onto a floured board and knead for 5 minutes or until dough is smooth and elastic.

Place dough in a warm greased bowl, turn so it is lightly greased all over, cover with a damp cloth and leave in a warm place to rise for $\frac{3}{4}$–1 hour or until doubled in bulk. Knead it lightly to knock out the air, pull sides to the center, turn it over, cover and let rise again for 30 minutes. Then add other ingredients called for in the individual recipe, and shape and bake coffeecake.

If dough is not to be used immediately, omit the last 30 minute period of rising, cover the top of the bowl tightly and keep dough in refrigerator for up to 48 hours if necessary. If dough rises to the top of the bowl, push it down again. When needed, transfer dough to a warm bowl and keep it at room temperature for 1 hour or longer until it has started to rise again. At this stage, dried fruit or other ingredients called for in the recipe should be added.

Easter Ring

2 cup quantity basic coffeecake dough
2 tablespoons butter, softened
$\frac{1}{4}$ cup sugar
$\frac{1}{3}$ cup raisins
1 teaspoon ground cinnamon (optional)

For decoration
soft icing (made with $\frac{1}{2}$ cup confectioners' sugar mixed with $1\frac{1}{2}$ teaspoons water)
8–12 walnut halves
8–12 candied cherries
little candied angelica (optional)

Method
After dough has risen twice, knead it lightly; turn out onto a floured board and roll out to a 16 X 9 inch rectangle. Dot the surface with the butter and sprinkle with sugar, raisins and cinnamon (if used). Roll up dough tightly, beginning at a long side and seal it by pinching the edges well together.

Curl dough around into a ring, seam underneath, and set on a greased baking sheet. Snip dough at 1 inch intervals with scissors, making each cut two-thirds through ring. Cover with a cloth and let stand in a warm place to rise for 30–40 minutes or until almost doubled in bulk. Set oven at hot (400°F).

Bake ring in heated oven for 25–30 minutes or until a skewer inserted comes out clean. Cool the ring a little, then transfer to a wire rack.

Make soft icing and brush it over the ring while still warm. Decorate with walnuts, cherries and leaves of angelica, if you like, and brush again lightly with icing.

Streusel Kuchen

4 cup quantity basic coffeecake dough

For streusel
5 tablespoons dark brown sugar
$1\frac{1}{2}$ tablespoons flour
1 teaspoon ground cinnamon
2 tablespoons melted butter
$\frac{1}{2}$ cup chopped walnuts

Large loaf pan (9 X 5 X 3 inches) or 8 inch springform pan

Method
Grease the pan well.

After dough has risen twice, knead it lightly and divide in half. Put half into the prepared pan and press it down well with your fist. Mix together all ingredients for the streusel and spread half on top of the dough. Cover with the remaining dough, press down again and sprinkle with the remaining streusel mixture.

Set oven at hot (400°F).

Let dough rise in a warm place for 30–40 minutes or until almost doubled in bulk, then bake in heated oven for 45–50 minutes or until the kuchen is well browned. Turn out onto a wire rack to cool.

For Easter ring, tightly roll up dough covered with butter, sugar, raisins and cinnamon

Snip dough, making a series of deep cuts, then let the dough rise in a warm place ▶

Decorate the baked ring — icing should be brushed on while Easter ring is still warm ▶

Easter ring is topped with soft icing and decorated with walnut halves, candied cherries and leaves cut from candied angelica

Apple Streusel Kuchen

2 cup quantity basic
  coffeecake dough

For apple mixture
3–4 Golden Delicious or other
  dessert apples
3–4 tablespoons butter
streusel (as for streusel
  kuchen – see page 18)

7–8 inch springform pan

It is important to use apples
that are not too tart and do
not become watery when
cooked.

Method
Grease the springform pan.
  Pare, core and quarter the
apples and cut each quarter in
half lengthwise. Sauté them
quickly in the butter for 3–4
minutes, turning often until
lightly browned, then cool.
  After dough has risen twice,
knead it lightly and press it
into the bottom of the pan.
Spoon apple slices on top of
dough.
  Prepare streusel and
sprinkle over the apple and
dough. Let stand in a warm
place to rise for 30–40
minutes or until almost
doubled in bulk. Set oven at
hot (400°F).
  Bake in heated oven for
about 45 minutes. If streusel
browns too quickly, turn down
the heat to moderately hot
(375°F) after 15 minutes and
continue baking about 30
minutes longer. Cool slightly,
take from the pan and serve
while still warm, or let it cool.

Kugelhopf

scant 1 cup lukewarm milk
1 package dry or 1 cake
  compressed yeast
3 cups flour
pinch of salt
2 tablespoons sugar
2 large or 3 small eggs,
  beaten to mix
$\frac{1}{2}$ cup melted butter
$\frac{1}{2}$ cup currants or golden
  raisins
$\frac{1}{2}$ cup raisins
$\frac{1}{2}$ cup whole blanched
  almonds, slivered
confectioners' sugar
  (for sprinkling) – optional

*7–8 inch kugelhopf pan or
  tube pan*

This coffeecake is so famous
in Germany that it gives its
name to a pan – a tube pan
with rounded base and fluted
sides.

Method
Sprinkle or crumble the yeast
over the milk and let stand
about 5 minutes until dissolved. Sift flour with salt into
a warm bowl, make a well in
the center, pour in the milk
and yeast mixture, the sugar,
eggs and the melted (but not
hot) butter. Work with the
hand to a smooth dough,
then beat with the hand for 5
minutes until dough is very
elastic; work in the dried
fruits.
  Thickly butter the pan and
press almonds around the
sides and base. Set oven at
hot (400°F).
  Transfer dough to pan – it
should half fill it. Cover with a
damp cloth and let rise in a
warm place for 30–40 minutes
or until dough is about $\frac{3}{4}$ inch
from top of pan.
  Stand the pan on a baking
sheet and bake in heated oven
for 50–60 minutes or until
kugelhopf is well browned

and a toothpick inserted in the
center comes out clean. If the
top begins to get very brown
during baking, cover kugelhopf with a sheet of foil, turn
down oven to moderate
(350°F) and continue baking.
  Let stand for a few moments
before turning out onto a wire
rack to cool completely. If you
like, sprinkle with confectioners' sugar before serving.
Watchpoint: for a light, airy
kugelhopf, prepare as above;
for a finer-textured cake, after
beating dough, let rise in a
warm place until almost
doubled in bulk, work lightly
to knock out air, add dried
fruits and continue as above.

*Transfer kugelhopf dough into
the prepared pan and let rise
in a warm place*

Stollen

2 cup quantity basic
  coffeecake dough
$\frac{1}{3}$ cup blanched almonds,
  chopped
3 tablespoons candied cherries,
  quartered
3 tablespoons chopped citron
  peel
$\frac{1}{4}$ cup raisins
$\frac{1}{4}$ cup golden raisins
grated rind of $\frac{1}{2}$ lemon
3 tablespoons butter, softened
soft icing (made with $\frac{1}{2}$ cup
  confectioners' sugar mixed
  with $1\frac{1}{2}$ teaspoons water) or
  confectioners' sugar
  (for topping)

Method
After dough has risen twice,
knead it lightly and turn out
onto a floured board. Add
almonds, candied and dried
fruits and the lemon rind;
knead in fruit and pat or roll
out dough to an oval about 10
inches long and 8 inches wide.
  Spread with two-thirds of
the butter, fold in half lengthwise and shape into a crescent.
Press the edges firmly
together.
  Place stollen on a greased
baking sheet, melt remaining butter and brush top of
stollen with it. Set oven at hot
(400°F).
  Leave stollen in a warm
place to rise for 30–40
minutes or until almost
doubled in bulk. Bake in
heated oven for 30–35
minutes or until browned.
Turn out onto a wire rack to
cool.
  Make soft icing and pour
over the top of the stollen
while still warm. Alternatively,
let stollen cool and sprinkle it
generously with confectioners'
sugar.

Sprinkle the finished kugelhopf with confectioners' sugar for serving

Hungarian Coffeecake

4 cups flour
1 teaspoon salt
$\frac{1}{4}$ cup sugar
$1\frac{1}{2}$ cups lukewarm milk
1 package dry or 1 cake
    compressed yeast
$\frac{1}{4}$ cup melted butter
1 egg, beaten to mix

For filling
$\frac{3}{4}$ cup sugar
1 teaspoon ground cinnamon
$\frac{1}{2}$ cup whole blanched almonds,
    finely chopped
$\frac{1}{2}$ cup melted butter
$\frac{1}{2}$ cup raisins

9 inch tube pan

Method
Sift flour with salt into a warm bowl. Add sugar to the lukewarm milk, sprinkle or crumble in the yeast and let stand 5 minutes until dissolved. Stir in the melted butter and beaten egg. Make a well in the center of the flour, add yeast mixture and work with the hand to a smooth dough. Turn out onto a floured board and knead the dough until it is very elastic. Place it in a greased bowl, cover with a damp cloth and let rise in a warm place for 1 hour or until doubled in bulk. Knead it lightly to knock out the air, cover and let rise again for about 30 minutes.

Turn out onto a floured board, knead lightly and divide into walnut-sized pieces. Cover with a cloth and let stand 15 minutes.

Set oven at moderately hot (375°F) and grease tube pan.

Mix sugar, cinnamon and chopped almonds together for the filling.

Shape pieces of dough into neat balls and roll them first in melted butter and then in the almond mixture. Place a layer of the balls so they barely touch each other in the bottom of the pan and sprinkle with raisins. Add another layer of balls, sprinkle with more raisins and press down lightly. Continue until all the dough and raisins are used. Cover with a damp cloth and let stand in a warm place for 30–40 minutes or until dough has risen almost to the top of the pan. Bake in heated oven for 35–40 minutes or until the coffeecake is well browned.

Loosen coffeecake from the pan, turn it upside down on a platter and let stand for the butter and sugar mixture to run down the sides. Serve warm or cold. Do not cut the coffeecake, but break it apart with 2 forks.

Easter Braid

2 cup quantity basic coffeecake
    dough
grated rind of $\frac{1}{2}$ lemon
1 teaspoon ground cinnamon
$\frac{1}{2}$ teaspoon ground nutmeg
$\frac{1}{2}$ cup currants or raisins
$\frac{1}{2}$ cup golden raisins

For topping
1 egg white, lightly beaten
2 tablespoons chopped candied
    green cherries
2 tablespoons chopped candied
    red cherries

Method
When making the basic dough, add the lemon rind and spices with the sugar. When the dough has risen twice, work in the currants or raisins and golden raisins.

Shape the dough into a cylinder and, leaving one end joined, cut it in three lengthwise. Braid it and turn under the loose ends.

Transfer the braid to a greased baking sheet, cover and let rise in a warm place for 30–40 minutes or until it is almost doubled in bulk.

Set oven at hot (400°F).

Brush the bread with lightly beaten egg white and bake in the heated oven for 25–30 minutes or until the bread sounds hollow when tapped. Brush again with beaten egg white 5 minutes before the end of cooking. Transfer the bread to a wire rack.

Mix the remaining egg white with the candied red and green cherries and spread this mixture on top of the bread while it is still hot. Serve warm or cold with butter.

Kugelhopf, baba and **savarin** coffeecakes are closely related. Babas are supposed to have been invented by Stanislaus Leszczynski, King of Poland, in 1609 when he sprinkled rum on his dry kugelhopf. He christened it Ali Baba and later the first name was dropped, leaving baba. In the 19th century, a French pastrycook omitted the currants from the dough, baked the cake in a plain ring mold and called it after the famous gourmet, Brillat-Savarin. This cake, too, lost its first name to become the liqueur-soaked coffeecake called savarin — see recipe in Volume 4.

Easter braid is topped with a mixture of chopped candied red and green cherries mixed with egg white

Hazelnut Bread

1½ cups flour
pinch of salt
½ cup butter
1 package dry or 1 cake
   compressed yeast
3 tablespoons lukewarm
   milk, mixed with
   2 tablespoons lukewarm
   water
2 tablespoons sugar
sugar (for sprinkling)

For filling
1 cup shelled hazelnuts,
   browned and ground
   (see page 12)
½ cup sugar
¾ cup sponge cake crumbs
1 small egg, beaten to mix with
   1 tablespoon water

Large loaf pan (9 X 5 X 3 inches)

Method
Sift flour and salt into a warm bowl and rub in 6 tablespoons of the butter with the fingertips until mixture resembles crumbs. Sprinkle or crumble yeast over the lukewarm milk and water, let stand about 5 minutes until dissolved and stir in the sugar. Make a well in the center of the flour, pour in yeast mixture and work with the hand to a fairly firm dough. Turn out onto a floured board and knead 5 minutes until dough is very smooth and elastic.

Transfer the dough to a buttered bowl, cover with a damp cloth and let stand in a warm place to rise for about 1 hour or until it is doubled in bulk.

Lightly grease the loaf pan.

Mix all ingredients for the filling together. On a floured board, knead lightly, then roll out dough to a 20 X 9 inch rectangle, spread with filling and roll up from each short end to meet in the center. Set in the prepared pan, cover with a damp cloth and let rise in a warm place for 30–40 minutes or until dough is almost doubled in bulk. Set oven at hot (400°F).

Bake in heated oven for 10 minutes, then lower heat to moderately low (325°F) and continue baking for about 50 minutes longer or until bread is well browned and a toothpick inserted in the center comes out clean. Cool on a wire rack.

Melt remaining butter, brush top of bread with it and sprinkle generously with sugar.

Babas au Rhum

1½ cups flour
1 teaspoon salt
1 tablespoon sugar
1 package dry or 1 cake
   compressed yeast
3 tablespoons lukewarm water
3 eggs, beaten to mix
½ cup butter, softened
½ cup currants or raisins

For syrup
¼ cup rum
1½ cups sugar
2 cups water

12–14 dariole molds

Method
Sift flour into a warm bowl with salt and sugar. Sprinkle or crumble yeast over the lukewarm water and let stand 5 minutes or until dissolved. Make a well in the center of the flour, pour in yeast mixture and add eggs. Work to a smooth dough with the hand, then beat 5 minutes or until dough is very smooth and elastic, raising it up with the fingers and letting it fall back into the bowl. Cover bowl with a damp cloth and let stand in a warm place for 45–60 minutes or until doubled in bulk.

Set oven at hot (400°F); thoroughly butter the molds. Beat butter into dough until very smooth. Mix in currants or raisins and spoon dough into molds to half fill them. Set them on a baking sheet, cover with a damp cloth and let rise in a warm place for 15–25 minutes or until dough almost reaches the top of the molds. Bake in heated oven for 20 minutes or until a toothpick inserted in the center comes out clean.

To make syrup: dissolve sugar in water over gentle heat, then boil rapidly for 5 minutes or until a drop of syrup tested between finger and thumb is sticky. Take from heat and stir in rum.

Turn babas out onto a wire rack placed over a large plate. Cool them for a few minutes, then spoon over the hot syrup; the plate will catch the excess syrup. Keep basting the babas, reheating the syrup, if necessary, until it has all been absorbed. The babas will swell a good deal and be very shiny. **Note**: if preparing babas ahead, do not add syrup, but sprinkle it over the babas just before serving.

Doughnuts

4 cups flour
½ teaspoon salt
¼ cup butter
1½–1¾ cups lukewarm milk
1 package dry or 1 cake
   compressed yeast
⅓ cup sugar
2 eggs, beaten to mix
deep fat (for frying)

To finish
¾ cup sugar
2 teaspoons ground cinnamon

*Doughnut cutter, or 2½–3 inch
and 1 inch cookie cutters*

Makes about 24 doughnuts.

Method
Sift flour and salt into a warm bowl. Add butter to 1½ cups of the lukewarm milk, sprinkle or crumble in the yeast and let stand about 5 minutes or until dissolved. Stir in sugar and eggs. Make a well in the center of the flour, pour in yeast mixture and work with the hand to a smooth dough, adding more milk if necessary.

Turn dough out onto a floured board and knead 5 minutes or until it is very smooth and elastic. Place dough in a warm greased bowl, cover with a damp cloth and let rise in a warm place for $\frac{3}{4}$–1 hour or until dough is doubled in bulk. Knead dough lightly to knock out the air and let rise again for 30 minutes.

Turn out dough onto a floured board, knead lightly and roll out to $\frac{1}{2}$ inch thickness. Cut out 2$\frac{1}{2}$–3 inch rounds with a doughnut cutter or, if using a cookie cutter, remove a 1 inch round from the center as well.

Transfer rings to a greased baking sheet, cover with a cloth; let stand in a warm place to rise for 20–25 minutes or until almost doubled in bulk.

Heat a pan of deep fat to 375°F on a fat thermometer. Using a slotted spatula, lower doughnuts, a few at a time, into the hot fat. Fry until golden brown on one side, turn and brown the other — about 3 minutes total cooking. Lift from the pan with the slotted spatula and drain on paper towels. Fry remaining doughnuts in the same way. When cool, drop them one by one into a bag with the sugar and cinnamon and shake until well coated.

Jelly Doughnuts

Roll out dough to $\frac{1}{4}$ inch thickness and cut 2$\frac{1}{2}$–3 inch rounds with a cookie cutter. Place a teaspoonful of jelly in the center of half the rounds, brush the edges with water and set the remaining dough rounds on top, pressing the edges well to seal them. Fry as for basic doughnut recipe and coat in sugar (without cinnamon).

Orange Doughnuts

When making dough, reduce quantity of milk by $\frac{1}{2}$ cup. Add grated rind of 1 orange and $\frac{1}{2}$ cup orange juice to the yeast mixture with the sugar and eggs.

Chocolate Doughnuts

Omit $\frac{1}{4}$ cup of the flour and add 1$\frac{1}{2}$ squares (1$\frac{1}{2}$ oz) semi-sweet chocolate, melted on a heatproof plate over a pan of hot water, to the yeast mixture with the sugar and eggs.

Jam Buns

2 cup quantity basic doughnut dough
about $\frac{1}{4}$ cup strawberry or raspberry jam, or redcurrant jelly
1 egg white, beaten until frothy
$\frac{1}{2}$ cup sugar cubes, coarsely crushed

Makes about 15–18 buns.

Method
Lightly grease a baking sheet.

After dough has risen twice, knead it lightly and divide into 15–18 equal pieces. Shape these into balls and place them 2 inches apart on pre-pared baking sheet. Cover with a cloth and let rise in a warm place for 30 minutes or until almost doubled in bulk. Set oven at hot (400°F).

Make a deep well in the center of each bun with your finger and fill with a teaspoon of jam or jelly. Brush buns with beaten egg white, sprinkle with crushed sugar and bake in heated oven for 12–15 minutes or until lightly browned.

Jelly doughnuts are coated with sugar for serving

A selection of Danish pastries: cartwheels and an envelope (at back), pinwheels and a comb (center) and three crescents (front)

DANISH PASTRIES

Deliciously light and flaky Danish pastries and French croissants are made with a yeast dough that is layered with butter and rolled like puff pastry. Danish pastries are usually made in various traditional shapes like cartwheels and pinwheels that are filled with almond paste, jam, apples, nuts and dried fruits. French croissants — always made in the same crescent shape — are not filled.

Basic Dough for Danish Pastries

3 cups flour
$\frac{1}{2}$ teaspoon salt
$\frac{1}{4}$ cup sugar
1 cup lukewarm milk
1 package dry or 1 cake
   compressed yeast
1 cup butter
1 egg, beaten to mix
1 egg, beaten with pinch of
   salt (for glaze)
soft icing (see recipe for
   stollen on page 20)

Makes 12 pastries of any shape.

Method
Sift flour with salt into a warm bowl. Stir sugar into the luke-warm milk, sprinkle or crumble yeast on top and let stand about 5 minutes or until dissolved. Melt $\frac{1}{4}$ cup of the butter and stir into yeast mixture with beaten egg.

Make a well in the flour, add yeast mixture and work with the hand to a smooth dough. Turn out onto a well floured board and knead 5 minutes or until very smooth and elastic. Place in a warm greased bowl, cover with a damp cloth and let rise in a warm place for 1 hour or until doubled in bulk. Turn out the dough onto a floured board and knead lightly to knock out the air. Roll out to a 16 X 6 inch rectangle and cover two-thirds of the dough with half the remaining butter, divided into small pieces. Fold one-third of the dough over the butter and fold the other third on top to make 3 layers. Turn dough so the open end faces you and roll again to a rectangle (as for flaky pastry). Fold in three, turn, then repeat rolling and folding once more.

Roll out again, add remaining butter in small pieces, fold in three and chill 15 minutes. Roll and fold twice more. Chill dough for 15 minutes.

Set oven at hot (400°F).

Roll out dough as described for the different kinds of pastries and set them on a greased baking sheet. Cover with a cloth and let rise in a warm place for 15 minutes or until almost doubled in bulk; brush with egg glaze and bake in heated oven for 10 minutes. Lower heat to moderate (350°F) and bake 10 minutes longer or until pastries are browned.

Transfer pastries to a wire rack and brush soft icing over them while still warm.

Dot two-thirds of dough with butter and fold into three

Complete six 'turns' before shaping. Pinwheel (below) is filled with jam

Cartwheels

Roll out dough to a large rectangle, $\frac{1}{4}$ inch thick. Spread carefully with a very thin layer of almond filling (see page 29), sprinkle with $\frac{1}{2}$ cup raisins and roll up like a jelly roll. Cut roll into $\frac{1}{2}$ inch slices and place, cut side down, on a greased baking sheet. Let rise as for basic dough, brush with beaten egg, sprinkle with blanched, chopped almonds and bake.

Envelopes

Roll out dough $\frac{1}{4}$ inch thick and cut into 4 inch squares. Spread with vanilla cream and fold the corners into the center; press the edges down lightly. Set envelopes on a greased baking sheet, let rise as for basic dough, brush them with beaten egg and bake.

Vanilla Cream

$\frac{1}{2}$ teaspoon vanilla
1 tablespoon flour
1 teaspoon cornstarch
1 tablespoon sugar
1 egg yolk
1 cup milk

Method
Mix flour, cornstarch and sugar with egg yolk and enough milk to make a smooth paste. Bring remaining milk to a boil, pour into mixture, blend and return to pan. Bring to a boil again, stirring, and simmer 1 minute. Take from heat, cover and cool; then stir in vanilla.

Crescents

Roll out dough to a large circle $\frac{1}{4}$ inch thick and cut it into 12 triangular sections. Spoon a little almond filling (see page 29) on each section and roll them up loosely, starting at the base of the triangle. Set them on a greased baking sheet and shape into crescents, pressing down the points. Let rise as for basic dough, brush crescents with beaten egg and bake.

Pinwheels, filled with jam, jelly or almond, are one of many Danish pastry variations

Pinwheels

Roll out dough $\frac{1}{4}$ inch thick and cut into 4 inch squares; cut diagonally from each corner to within $\frac{1}{2}$ inch of center. Put 1 teaspoon of jam, jelly or almond filling in the center and fold 4 alternate points to the center, pressing them down firmly. Transfer to a greased baking sheet, let rise as for basic dough, brush with beaten egg and bake.

Twists

Roll out dough to a rectangle 10 inches wide and $\frac{1}{4}$ inch thick. Cut in half to form two 5 inch strips. Spread 1 strip with almond filling and place the other strip on top, pressing it down well. Brush the top with beaten egg and sprinkle with blanched, chopped almonds. Cut into strips about 5 inches long and 1 inch wide, twist them and set on a greased baking sheet, pressing ends down well so twists do not unroll. Let rise as for basic dough, then bake.

Combs

Roll out dough to a long strip about 5 inches wide and $\frac{1}{4}$ inch thick.

Spoon almond or apple filling down one side only about 1 inch from one edge. Brush edge with beaten egg and fold the other side over top to enclose filling; press edges together well to seal them. Brush with beaten egg and sprinkle with blanched, chopped almonds and, if you like, with crushed cube sugar. Cut dough into pieces about 4 inches long and make 4–5 deep cuts in the folded side to expose the filling. Open the

slits slightly and place combs on a greased baking sheet. Let rise as for basic dough, and bake.

Almond Filling

$\frac{1}{3}$ cup whole blanched almonds, ground
$\frac{1}{2}$ cup sugar
little beaten egg
few drops of almond extract (optional)

This filling keeps well (wrapped in wax paper) for 1–2 weeks in refrigerator.

Method
Mix almonds and sugar together and bind with enough egg to make a soft paste. Flavor with a few drops of almond extract, if you like.

Apple Filling

3 tart apples
1 tablespoon butter
grated rind and juice of $\frac{1}{2}$ lemon
$\frac{1}{4}$ cup sugar

Pastries filled with apple filling can be brushed with apricot jam glaze instead of soft icing. This filling keeps well for 1–2 weeks in a covered container in the refrigerator.

Method
Wipe apples, core and slice them but do not pare. Spread butter around a saucepan, add apples and lemon rind and juice, cover and cook over low heat until apples are pulpy.

Work apples through a nylon strainer or purée in a blender; return to pan with sugar. Cook gently, stirring until thick. Cool completely before using.

French Croissants

4 cups flour
1 package dry or 1 cake compressed yeast
6 tablespoons lukewarm water
1 teaspoon salt
2 tablespoons sugar
1 cup butter
about 6 tablespoons milk
1 egg, beaten with pinch of salt (for glaze)

Makes about 32 croissants.

Method
Sift flour. Sprinkle or crumble yeast into the lukewarm water and let stand 5 minutes or until dissolved. Stir yeast mixture into about $\frac{1}{4}$ of the flour in a warm bowl to make a smooth soft dough. Roll it into a ball, cut a cross on top to help it rise and drop the ball into a large bowl of warm water (the water should feel just warm to the touch).

Mix remaining flour with salt and sugar. Work in half the butter with fingertips until mixture resembles crumbs, then stir in enough milk to make a dough that is soft but not sticky. Beat dough on a lightly floured board by lifting it 1–2 feet and throwing it down again on the board for 5 minutes or until it is very smooth and elastic.

When yeast ball has risen to the surface of the water and is almost doubled in size, drain with a slotted spatula and add to remaining dough. Put dough in a floured bowl, cover with a damp cloth and let stand overnight in the refrigerator. At the end of this time dough will be well risen and it may be necessary to push it down if it rises to the top of the bowl. When well chilled like this it is easy to handle. Place remaining butter between 2 sheets of wax paper and pound with a

rolling pin until it is pliable but not sticky. Shape into a 4 inch square cake.

Work dough lightly to knock out any air, then roll out to a 14 X 5 inch rectangle. Place butter in the center, fold one-third of the dough over the butter and fold the other third on top to make 3 layers. Turn folded dough so one of the open ends faces towards you. Roll out again, fold over as before and turn. Repeat once more. Wrap in a plastic bag and chill 15 minutes or until firm. Repeat the rolling and folding twice more. Chill again 15 minutes or until firm.

Set oven at hot (425°F).

To shape croissants: roll out dough to a rectangle one-eighth inch thick, cut into 4 inch squares and cut squares in half diagonally. Roll up, starting from the base of the triangle, curve the ends, pressing points down well; set on a lightly floured baking sheet. Cover with a cloth and let rise in a warm place for 20–25 minutes or until almost doubled in bulk.

Brush with egg glaze and bake in heated oven for 5 minutes. Turn down heat to moderately hot (375°F) and bake for 10 minutes or until browned. Cool on a wire rack.

The recipe for **croissants** originated in Budapest in 1686 when the city was being besieged by Turks, who tunneled under walls in an attempt to break the siege. They were overheard by bakers working at night, who raised the alarm. The city was saved and the bakers were granted the privilege of making a special pastry, shaped like the crescent moon on the Turkish flag.

BRIOCHES

Brioche dough is soft and almost silky to the touch and the finished bread is rich, with a light texture and a soft brown crust. The proportion of eggs and butter can vary — the richest dough is used for breakfast rolls and bread and a plainer mixture can be made into sweet rolls and topped with soft icing.

The preliminary mixing of the yeast, with a little flour and water, and the rising in a bowl of warm water is characteristic of rich French yeast doughs like brioches and croissants. The brioche shape of a ball crowned by another smaller ball is also characteristic.

Place yeast and flour mixture in a bowl of warm water

Add risen yeast mixture to butter, flour and egg dough

Small Brioches

For 5 cup quantity
5 cups flour
2 packages dry or 2 cakes
    compressed yeast
$\frac{1}{2}$ cup lukewarm water
2 tablespoons sugar
1 teaspoon salt
6 eggs
$1\frac{1}{2}$ cups butter, softened
flour (for sprinkling)
1 egg, beaten with
    1 tablespoon milk and
    pinch of salt (for glaze)

16—18 fluted brioche pans

Method
Sift flour. Sprinkle or crumble yeast over lukewarm water and let stand about 5 minutes or until dissolved. Stir yeast mixture into about $\frac{1}{4}$ of the flour in a warm bowl to make a soft dough. Roll into a ball, cut a cross in the top to help it rise and drop into a large bowl of warm water (the water should feel just warm to the touch).

Make a well in the remaining flour and add sugar, salt and eggs. Mix to a dough that is soft and slightly sticky. Beat the dough on a lightly floured board, by lifting it 1—2 feet and throwing it down again on the board for 5 minutes or until it is very smooth and elastic. If you like, this beating can be done in an electric mixer using a dough hook.

Work butter into dough until smooth. When yeast ball has risen to the surface of the water and is almost doubled in size, drain with a slotted spatula and add to the dough. Cut and fold the mixture carefully then knead into a large ball — it should be soft, but not too sticky (brioche dough should be softer at this stage than croissant dough).

Transfer to a warm but-

Shape the small brioches, place them in buttered pans and let rise in a warm place until almost doubled in bulk before baking

tered bowl, cover with a damp cloth and let rise in a warm place for $1\frac{1}{2}$—2 hours or until doubled in bulk. Knead lightly to knock out the air, pull sides to center and turn over. Cover with a damp cloth and chill 6—7 hours or overnight in refrigerator. At the end of this time dough will be well risen; it may be necessary to push it down if it has risen to the top of the bowl. When well chilled it is easy to handle.

Butter the brioche pans.

Knead dough lightly to knock out air, then divide into 16—18 pieces. Pinch off one-third of each piece of dough and shape both large and small pieces into balls. Set a large ball in the base of each brioche pan, cut a deep cross in the top and crown it with a smaller ball or 'head' of dough. Set oven at hot (425°F).

Let brioches rise in a warm

place for 25—30 minutes or until almost doubled in bulk, brush with egg glaze and bake in heated oven for 15—20 minutes or until well browned.

Cool a few moments in the pans, then turn out brioches and cool on a wire rack.

Watchpoint: the 'heads' of brioches often slip sideways or subside into the lower part of the dough. To help prevent this, the shaped brioches can be stored in the refrigerator overnight then, if necessary, put to rise in a warm place just before baking.

Split small freshly-baked brioches in half and spread with unsalted butter for breakfast

Brioche Loaf

Follow the recipe for small brioches. After leaving dough in refrigerator 6–7 hours or overnight, knead it lightly.

If using loaf pans, divide dough in half, shape into 2 oblongs, place them in 2 medium loaf pans ($8\frac{1}{2}$ X $4\frac{1}{2}$ X $2\frac{1}{2}$ inches each). Set on a baking sheet and let rise in a warm place for 30–40 minutes or until almost doubled in bulk. Brush with beaten egg and decorate with slices of candied orange, lemon and citron peel and halved candied cherries. Bake in a hot oven (400°F) for 35–45 minutes or until brioches are well browned and start pulling away from sides of pan. Cool a few moments in the pans, then turn out and cool completely on a wire rack. While still warm brush with soft icing (see recipe for stollen, page 20).

If using large fluted brioche loaf pans, shape dough into 2 large balls and crown them with 2 small balls, as for small brioches. Let rise as in loaf pans and brush with beaten egg glaze before baking. Do not add candied fruit or icing.

Pâté de Foie Gras en Brioche

$2\frac{1}{2}$ cup quantity dough as for small brioches
long cylindrical can (11 oz) pâté de foie gras
1 egg, beaten with pinch of salt (for glaze)

Large loaf pan (9 X 5 X 3 inches)

Method

Make brioche dough to the stage where it has been chilled 6–7 hours or overnight and is easy to handle.

Grease loaf pan.

Knead dough lightly and roll out on a floured board to 9 X 7 inch rectangle. Set block of pâté lengthwise on center of dough and roll dough around it. Seal edges well. Turn it over so the seam is underneath and place in prepared pan. Cover with a damp cloth and let rise in a warm place for 25–30 minutes or until almost doubled in bulk. Set oven at hot (400°F).

Brush with egg glaze and bake in heated oven for 30–35 minutes or until brioche is well browned and starts pulling away from sides of pan. Turn out onto a wire rack to cool. To serve, cut in $\frac{3}{4}$ inch slices, discarding the ends, so each person has a serving of foie gras.

Saucisson en Brioche

Follow the recipe for pâté de foie gras en brioche, using $1–1\frac{1}{2}$ lb Polish Kielbasa or French garlic sausage. Simmer the sausage in water to cover for 15–20 minutes, cool and remove skin before rolling in dough. The baking time is the same as for pâté.

Grapfruit

$2\frac{1}{2}$ cup quantity dough as for small brioches
$\frac{1}{2}$–$\frac{3}{4}$ cup dark cherry, strawberry, or other whole fruit preserves
deep fat (for frying)
confectioners' sugar (for sprinkling)

$2\frac{1}{2}$–3 inch cookie cutter;
fat thermometer

Grapfruit are a kind of very rich doughnut, but made with brioche dough. Makes 10–12.

Method

Make brioche dough to the stage where it has been chilled 6–7 hours or overnight and is easy to handle.

Knead dough lightly and roll out on a floured board to about $\frac{1}{2}$ inch thickness.

Cut out rounds with cookie cutter. Put a teaspoon of the actual fruit from the preserves in the center of each one, brush around the edge with water, then pinch into balls. Set on a greased baking sheet, cover with a cloth and leave in a warm place for about 5 minutes or until dough is just beginning to rise.

Heat fat to 360°F on a fat thermometer and add the grapfruit, a few at a time. Fry them for 5–8 minutes, slowly increasing the heat to 380°F, until they are puffed and brown. Turn occasionally as the grapfruit swell. Lift out with a slotted spoon and drain well on paper towels. Fry remaining grapfruit in the same way. When they are cool, drop them one by one into a bag with the sugar and shake until well coated.

Brioche Sweet Rolls

3 cups flour
$\frac{1}{2}$ teaspoon salt
1 package dry or 1 cake compressed yeast
3–4 tablespoons lukewarm water
$\frac{1}{4}$ cup sugar
2 eggs
2–3 tablespoons milk (optional)
$\frac{1}{3}$–$\frac{1}{2}$ cup butter, softened
$\frac{1}{2}$ cup apricot, strawberry or other jam

To finish
soft icing (see recipe for stollen on page 20), or $\frac{1}{4}$ cup thin apricot jam glaze, or milk glaze (made with $1\frac{1}{2}$ tablespoons sugar mixed with 1 tablespoon warm milk until dissolved)

Makes 12–16 rolls.

Method

Sift flour with salt. Sprinkle or crumble yeast over the lukewarm water and let stand 5 minutes or until dissolved. Stir yeast mixture into about $\frac{1}{4}$ of the flour in a warm bowl to make a soft dough. Roll into a ball, cut a cross in the top to help it rise and drop into a large bowl of warm water (the water should feel just warm to the touch).

Add sugar to remaining flour, make a well in the center, add eggs and work with the hand to a soft dough, adding milk if necessary — the mixture should fall from the spoon without being liquid.

Beat dough thoroughly with your hand, lifting it and letting it fall back into the bowl, for 5 minutes or until it is very smooth and elastic. If you like, this beating can be done in an electric mixer using a dough hook. Work the butter into dough until very smooth.

When yeast ball has risen to

the surface of the water and has almost doubled in size, drain with a slotted spatula and add to dough. Cut and fold mixture together carefully, then knead into a large ball — it should be soft but not too sticky. Transfer to a buttered bowl, cover and chill in the refrigerator for 3–4 hours or overnight. At the end of this time the dough will be well risen. If leaving overnight, it may be necessary to push dough down when it has risen to the top of the bowl. When well chilled like this it is easy to handle.

Grease a baking sheet.

To shape into rolls: knead dough lightly, then roll out on a lightly floured board to a 15 X 10 inch rectangle. Spread with jam and roll up like a jelly roll. Press edge down firmly and cut the roll into $\frac{3}{4}$ inch slices. Lay them, cut side down, on prepared baking sheet. Cover with a cloth and let rise in a warm place for 15–20 minutes or until almost doubled in bulk. Set oven at hot (400°F).

Bake in heated oven for 10–15 minutes or until browned. Transfer to a wire rack immediately and, when slightly cooled, brush with soft icing. Alternatively, instead of icing, brush the rolls with thin apricot jam glaze or with a little milk glaze just before the end of baking and bake 2–3 minutes longer until shiny. Cool on a wire rack.

Pandolce
(Italian Sweet Bread)

2 cakes compressed yeast or
  2 packages dry yeast
$\frac{1}{2}$ cup lukewarm milk
4 cups flour
$\frac{1}{2}$ teaspoon salt
$\frac{1}{2}$ cup sugar
5 eggs
2 tablespoons orange flower
  water
$\frac{3}{4}$ cup butter, softened
$\frac{1}{2}$ cup pine nuts
$\frac{1}{2}$ cup raisins
$\frac{1}{2}$ cup golden raisins
$\frac{1}{2}$ cup chopped candied citron
  peel
confectioners' sugar
  (for sprinkling)
slices of candied citron peel
  (for decoration) – optional
8 inch springform pan

Method
Sprinkle or crumble the yeast over the milk and leave 5 minutes or until dissolved.

Sift the flour with the salt into a bowl, stir in the sugar and make a well in the center. Add the yeast mixture, eggs and orange flower water and mix with the hand to a smooth dough. Beat with the hand for 5 minutes or until the dough is smooth and elastic. Work in the butter, pine nuts, raisins and candied peel. Cover the bowl with a damp cloth and let rise in a warm place for $1\frac{1}{2}$–2 hours or until the dough is doubled in bulk. Grease the cake pan.

When risen, knead the dough lightly to knock out the air, transfer it to the prepared pan, cover and let rise again in a warm place until it is almost doubled in bulk.

Set oven at moderately hot (375°F).

When risen, bake the bread in the heated oven for 50–60 minutes or until the bread sounds hollow when tapped. Transfer it to a wire rack to cool.

Before serving, sprinkle with confectioners' sugar and decorate with slices of candied citron peel, if you like.

Pandolce is decorated with slices of candied citron peel

COOKING WITH LEFTOVERS

There are so many delicious dishes based on cooked ingredients that leftovers need never be obviously left over. It is important to garnish attractively a dish made from leftovers; if pieces of cooked meat or poultry are too small to cut into neat slices, use a recipe that calls for them to be ground. Whatever the recipe, cooked ingredients should never be re-cooked but only heated through until very hot. Meat may be left to stand in a hot sauce for a short time to absorb the flavors. Reheating at too high a heat will make leftovers tough and tasteless.

Superbly creamy croquettes or richly spiced curry can be made with leftover cooked meat or poultry, but if these are stale or dry to begin with, it is not worth adding good ingredients to them. When using leftovers that are already highly seasoned, for instance meat in a barbecue sauce, do not add more seasoning before tasting the mixture.

Beef with zucchini and tomatoes

Pain Farci
(Stuffed Bread)

1 lb unsliced loaf of white
   bread
1½–2 cups (about ¾ lb) cooked
   diced beef, lamb or ham
3 tablespoons softened butter
1 clove of garlic, crushed

For salpicon
3–4 chicken livers, or 1 lamb's
   or small veal kidney
2 tablespoons oil
2 onions, thinly sliced
2 mushrooms, thinly sliced
1½ tablespoons flour
1 cup stock
salt and pepper
1 tablespoon chopped parsley
2 tomatoes, peeled, sliced
   and seeded

Method

Cream the butter and beat in
the crushed garlic. Cut a thin
horizontal slice from the top
of the loaf and scoop out the
soft inside of the loaf, leaving
'walls' about ½ inch thick.
Brush the hollowed bread and
the 'lid' with garlic butter.

To make salpicon: cut the
core from the kidney, if using,
and sauté the kidney or liver
in the oil for 2–3 minutes or
until browned. Take out and
slice. Add the onion and
mushrooms to the pan and fry
until beginning to brown. Stir
in the flour and cook until
browned, then pour in the
stock and bring to a boil, stirring. Season, replace the
slices of kidney or liver and
simmer 5–6 minutes. Take
from the heat, add the diced
meat, parsley and tomatoes,
mix well, taste for seasoning
and put into the loaf. Replace
the top, leaving it half open.
Wrap foil around the loaf, set
in a baking dish and bake in a
moderate oven (350°F) for
30–40 minutes or until the
salpicon is very hot and the
loaf is crisp.

Remove from foil; cut the
loaf into thick slices and serve
at once with salad or a green
vegetable.

Beef with Zucchini and Tomatoes

1½–2 cups cooked beef, cut in
   small cubes
3 zucchini, sliced
4 tomatoes, peeled, seeded
   and cut in strips
1 cup (¼ lb) mushrooms,
   quartered (optional)
1 cup leftover gravy or 1 cup
   espagnole sauce
salt and pepper
2 tablespoons oil
¼ cup grated Gruyère or
   Cheddar cheese

Method

Simmer the mushrooms, if
using, in the gravy or espagnole sauce for 1–2 minutes or
until tender; add the beef.
Parboil the zucchini in boiling
salted water for 4–5 minutes
and drain.

Arrange half the tomatoes
and half the zucchini in the
bottom of a shallow baking
dish, sprinkle with seasoning
and a little oil and spread the
beef mixture on top. Cover
with the remaining tomatoes
and zucchini, sprinkle again
with seasoning and the
remaining oil.

Scatter over the grated
cheese and bake in a
moderate oven (350°F) for
15–20 minutes or until the
tomatoes and zucchini are
tender and the cheese is
browned.

Espagnole Sauce

6 tablespoons oil
1 onion, finely diced
1 carrot, finely diced
1 stick celery, finely diced
3 tablespoons flour
1 teaspoon tomato paste
2 tablespoons chopped
   mushroom stalks, or
   1 mushroom, chopped
5 cups well-flavored brown
   stock
bouquet garni
salt and pepper

Method

In a saucepan, heat oil and
add diced vegetables (there
should be no more than 6
tablespoons of vegetables in
all). Lower the heat and cook
gently until the vegetables are
transparent and about to start
browning. They will shrink
slightly at this point.

Stir in the flour and brown
it slowly, stirring occasionally
with a wire whisk or metal
spoon and scraping the flour
well from the bottom of the
pan. When it is brown, take
from heat and cool slightly.
Watchpoint: the flour should
be cooked until dark brown,
but do not allow it to burn.

Stir in the tomato paste,
chopped mushroom, 4 cups
cold stock, bouquet garni and
seasoning.

Bring to a boil, whisking
constantly, partly cover the
pan and cook gently for 35–
40 minutes. During this time
skim off any scum which rises
to the surface. Then add half
the remaining stock, bring
again to a boil and skim.
Simmer 5 minutes, add the
remaining stock, bring to a
boil and skim again. (The cold
stock accelerates the rising of
scum and helps to clear
sauce.)

Cook 5 minutes longer,
then strain, pressing vegetables gently to extract the
juice. Clean pan and return
sauce to it. Partly cover pan
and continue to simmer sauce
until it is very glossy and the
consistency of heavy cream.

Mazagrans

1½ cups (½ lb) cooked duck or
   pork, ground
2 medium onions, finely
   chopped
2 tablespoons butter
1 cup gravy or espagnole sauce
1 teaspoon Worcestershire
   sauce
salt and pepper
3–4 potatoes, boiled, mashed
   with ¼ cup milk and
   2–3 tablespoons butter and
   seasoned
1–2 tablespoons melted butter
4 gherkin pickles (for garnish)

4 heatproof baking dishes

Method

Fry the onion in 2 tablespoons
butter until golden brown.
Add to the duck or pork with
enough gravy or sauce to
moisten the mixture. Add the
Worcestershire sauce and
taste for seasoning.

Butter the baking dishes,
spread a thin layer of mashed
potato in the bottom of each
and fill with the meat mixture.
Spread the remaining potato
on top and smooth with a
metal spatula. Mark with the
end of a knife handle in a lattice pattern or in a figure 8
and brush with melted butter.
Bake in a hot oven (400°F) for
10–15 minutes until hot and
browned.

Slice each gherkin pickle
thinly almost to the end and
fan out the slices; place 1 on
each baking dish. Serve hot.

Beef with Red Wine and Prunes

8–10 slices of cooked beef
$\frac{1}{2}$ cup red wine
$1\frac{1}{2}$ cups ($\frac{1}{2}$ lb) dried prunes, pitted and soaked overnight in tea
4 large onions, sliced
2 tablespoons butter
$\frac{1}{4}$ cup stock
salt and pepper
1–2 tablespoons Dijon-style mustard
maître d'hôtel potatoes (for serving)

Method

Put prunes in a pan with just enough soaking liquid to cover, cover the pan and simmer 10 minutes. Add half the wine and continue cooking, uncovered, until all the liquid has evaporated and the prunes are glazed. Fry the onions gently in the butter until golden brown, add the remaining wine and the stock, season well and simmer 3–4 minutes.

Spread the slices of beef with mustard and arrange them in a shallow baking dish. Spoon over the onion mixture and heat the meat in a moderate oven (350°F) for 7–10 minutes or until very hot. Garnish the dish with prunes and serve maître d'hôtel potatoes separately.

Prunes soaked in tea have better color and flavor, though the taste of tea is lost during cooking. The tea should be freshly brewed.

Maître d'Hôtel Potatoes

Scrub $1\frac{1}{2}$ lb potatoes and then boil them for 15–20 minutes until tender but firm. Drain, dry and peel them and cut into three-eighth inch slices; arrange in a hot shallow ovenproof dish.

Melt 3 tablespoons butter in a pan, add 1 chopped shallot, cover pan and cook over a low heat for 2–3 minutes or until shallot is soft. Take the pan from the heat and add 2 tablespoons chopped parsley and plenty of salt and pepper. Pour this mixture over the potatoes and serve.

Molded Beef

3 cups (1 lb) pieces cooked beef
$\frac{1}{4}$ cup browned breadcrumbs
1 onion, finely chopped
$1\frac{1}{2}$ cups fresh white breadcrumbs
1 tablespoon chopped parsley
salt
black pepper, freshly ground
4 eggs, beaten to mix
$\frac{1}{2}$ cup stock or water
tomato sauce (for serving)

Charlotte mold or soufflé dish ($1\frac{1}{2}$ quart capacity)

Method

Grease the mold or dish and sprinkle it thickly with the browned breadcrumbs. Set oven at moderate (350°F).

Discard any skin or gristle from the meat and work it twice through the fine blade of a grinder. Blanch the onion for 1 minute in boiling salted water, drain it and mix with the fresh breadcrumbs, parsley and plenty of seasoning. Stir in the beaten eggs and stock, then add the meat and mix well. Fill the mixture into the prepared mold, press it down firmly and cover with buttered foil. Bake in the heated oven for 40 minutes or until a skewer inserted in the center for 1 minute is hot to the touch when withdrawn.

Turn out onto a hot serving dish, spoon around a little tomato sauce and serve the rest separately.

Miroton of Beef

10–12 thin slices cooked beef
2 medium-sized onions, finely chopped
2 tablespoons beef drippings or oil
1 teaspoon flour
1 cup stock
$\frac{1}{3}$ cup white wine or cider
1 clove of garlic, crushed
1 bay leaf
salt
black pepper, freshly ground
4–5 boiled potatoes
squeeze of lemon juice
3 tablespoons fresh or dry white breadcrumbs
1 tablespoon butter

Method

In a skillet fry the onions in the drippings or oil until just beginning to brown, stir in the flour and cook until brown. Add the stock, wine or cider, garlic, bay leaf and seasoning and bring to a boil, stirring; cover, simmer 10 minutes, then let cool.

Add the beef to the sauce, heat the mixture gently to tepid and let stand 10–15 minutes.

Watchpoint: do not add the cooked beef to boiling sauce because the heat will toughen the surface of the meat and it will not absorb the flavor of the sauce.

Cut the potatoes in $\frac{1}{4}$-inch slices and arrange them, overlapping, standing up in a circle around the edge of a heat-proof serving dish. Arrange the beef inside, add lemon juice to the sauce, taste for seasoning and spoon over the meat. Sprinkle with breadcrumbs, dot with butter and bake in a hot oven (400°F) for 10 minutes or until browned.

Sauce Gribiche

3 hard-cooked eggs
$\frac{1}{2}$ teaspoon dry mustard
salt and pepper
1 cup olive oil
5 tablespoons vinegar (wine or tarragon)
2 tablespoons chopped gherkin pickles
2 tablespoons capers
1 tablespoon chopped parsley
1 teaspoon tarragon
2 teaspoons chopped chives

Serve sauce Gribiche with cold turkey or chicken or with cold meats.

Method
Cut the eggs in half, scoop out the yolks and work them through a sieve; finely slice the whites.

In a small bowl beat the egg yolks with the mustard, salt and pepper and 2 teaspoons olive oil. Add the remaining oil a little at a time, beating constantly as for mayonnaise—the sauce should be smooth and fairly thick; stir in the vinegar. If you like, the sauce can be made up to this point in the blender. Stir in remaining ingredients with egg whites and season to taste.

Cold Ham Soufflé

1 cup ($\frac{1}{2}$ lb) cooked lean ham
béchamel sauce, made with
   1 tablespoon butter,
   1 tablespoon flour and $\frac{3}{4}$ cup milk (infused with slice of onion, 6 peppercorns, blade of mace and bay leaf)
1 teaspoon tomato paste
1 tablespoon sherry
1 envelope gelatin
1$\frac{1}{4}$ cups aspic (made with 1 can consommé and $\frac{1}{2}$ envelope gelatin)
salt and pepper
2 egg whites
$\frac{3}{4}$ cup heavy cream, whipped until it holds a soft shape
1 cucumber, thinly sliced (for garnish)

Soufflé dish (1 quart capacity)

Method
Prepare soufflé dish by tying around a paper collar to extend 2–3 inches above the level of the dish. Make béchamel sauce and cool. Work ham twice through the fine blade of a grinder, then pound it in a mortar and pestle, work through a sieve and stir in béchamel sauce. Alternatively, work the ham in a blender with a little of the cool béchamel sauce, then stir in remaining sauce. Stir in tomato paste and sherry.

Sprinkle gelatin over $\frac{1}{2}$ cup of the cool but still liquid aspic, let stand 5 minutes until soft and dissolve over a pan of hot water. Stir into the ham mixture, season to taste and chill in the refrigerator or over a bowl of ice water, stirring occasionally until on the point of setting.

Whip egg whites until they hold a stiff peak. When mixture starts to set, fold in the whipped cream, then the egg whites and pour into the prepared soufflé dish. Chill at least 2 hours or until set.

Spoon a thin layer of the remaining cool but still liquid aspic over the soufflé. Chill until set and arrange sliced cucumber on top. Pour over a little more aspic and chill again until set. Pour over the remaining aspic and chill thoroughly.

Just before serving, peel off the paper collar.

Ham Pilaf

1$\frac{1}{2}$ cups ($\frac{1}{2}$ lb) cooked sliced ham or corned beef, cut in strips
6 tablespoons butter
2 onions, sliced
3 tomatoes, peeled, sliced and seeded
$\frac{1}{4}$ cup ketchup
1$\frac{1}{4}$ cups rice, boiled, drained, and spread out to dry
1 package frozen peas, cooked according to package directions and drained
salt
black pepper, freshly ground

Method
Melt half the butter in a pan, add the onions and fry slowly until beginning to brown. Add the tomatoes, cover and continue frying 4–5 minutes until just cooked. Add the ham or corned beef and ketchup.

Melt the remaining butter in a skillet, add the rice and peas and cook over medium heat, tossing with 2 forks. When hot, stir in the meat and tomato mixture, taste for seasoning and continue tossing until very hot; serve at once.

Curried Lamb

8–10 slices of cooked lamb, trimmed of fat

For curry sauce
1 large onion, sliced
1 large tart apple, pared, cored and sliced
2 tablespoons butter or oil
1 tablespoon curry powder (or to taste)
1 tablespoon flour
2 cups stock
pinch of salt
2 tomatoes, peeled, seeded and cut in wedges
2 tablespoons mango or other chutney
1 tablespoon golden raisins (optional)

This is not a curry in the Indian tradition, but a European-style dish with a curry-flavored sauce.

Method
To make curry sauce: fry the onion and apple slices in the butter or oil until golden. Add the curry powder to taste and cook gently for 3–4 minutes. Take from the heat, stir in the flour and pour on the stock. Bring to a boil, stirring, add salt and simmer 10 minutes. Then add tomatoes, chutney, and raisins if you like, and simmer 10–15 minutes longer or until the sauce is fairly thick.

Put the meat in a flame-proof dish or casserole, spoon over the curry sauce, shake the dish or casserole to mix in the sauce, cover and bake in a moderately low oven (325°F) or heat very gently on top of the stove for 20–30 minutes or until the curry is very hot.
Watchpoint: do not boil the sauce or the meat will become tough — it should stand in the hot sauce to absorb the flavor.

Serve with boiled rice and fresh chutney.

Macaroni pie can be made with leftover cooked meat, poultry or fish

Veal Salad

6–8 slices (about 1 lb) roast
   veal
1 lb small new potatoes
½ cup vinaigrette dressing
12–16 ripe olives, pitted and
   chopped
2 tablespoons mixed chopped
   herbs (tarragon, chives,
   basil, parsley)

For dressing
1½ teaspoons paprika
1 clove of garlic, crushed with
   ¼ teaspoon salt
¾ cup sour cream
salt, sugar or lemon juice
   (to taste)

Method
Scrub or peel potatoes and
cook in boiling salted water
for 15–20 minutes or until just
tender. Drain and slice them
while still warm and mix with
the vinaigrette dressing.

Cut the cold roast veal into
strips, mix with the potatoes,
olives, and herbs and pile in a
salad bowl or serving dish.

To make dressing: mix
paprika with crushed garlic
and stir in the sour cream.
Season to taste with salt,
sugar or lemon juice, as you
like. Spoon this dressing over
veal salad about 15 minutes
before serving.

Macaroni Pie

½ lb macaroni
1½–2 cups cooked ham,
   chicken, turkey or fish, cut
   in strips
2 cups mornay sauce, made
   with 3 tablespoons butter,
   3 tablespoons flour, 2 cups
   milk, ½ cup grated Parmesan
   or Gruyère cheese and
   1 teaspoon prepared mustard
½ cup grated Parmesan or
   Gruyère cheese
   (for sprinkling)

For chicken, turkey or fish
¼ cup white wine or
   1 tablespoon lemon juice
2 teaspoons chopped tarragon
   or oregano

Method
If using chicken, turkey or fish,
mix them with white wine or
lemon juice and the herbs and
let marinate 1–2 hours.

Break the macaroni in half
if it is long and cook in boiling,
salted water for 10–12 minutes or until just tender ('al
dente'). Make the mornay
sauce and season well.

Drain the macaroni, rinse
with hot water, return to the
pan and add the sauce. Stir
gently to mix and spread half
in a buttered baking dish.
Spread the ham, chicken,
turkey or fish on top and cover
with remaining macaroni.
Sprinkle the top with grated
cheese and bake in a hot oven
(400°F) for 15 minutes or
until golden brown.

Stuffed Tomatoes

4 large even-sized tomatoes
¾ cup cooked beef, lamb or
   pork, ground
¼ cup butter
1 medium onion, finely
   chopped
3 tablespoons fresh white
   breadcrumbs
salt and pepper
2 tablespoons ketchup
¼ teaspoon thyme
¼ teaspoon basil or oregano
2 tablespoons meat gravy or
   stock
4 slices of white bread,
   toasted and crusts removed

This serves 4 people as an
appetizer; double the quantities in the recipe to serve as
an entrée.

Method
Cut a slice from one end (not
stalk end) of the tomatoes
and scoop out the seeds with
a teaspoon. Strain the juice
from the seeds and reserve.

In a small pan melt 2 tablespoons butter, add the onion
and cook until golden brown.
Stir into the ground meat with
the breadcrumbs and season
well. Mix the ketchup with the
reserved tomato juice and stir
into the meat mixture with a
fork. Add the herbs and gravy
or stock.

Fill the tomatoes with this
stuffing, piling it up well, and
replace the lids on a slant.
Butter the toast, set a tomato
on each piece, cover with buttered foil and bake in a
moderately hot oven (375°F)
for 15–20 minutes or until the
tomatoes are just cooked.

*Scoop out seeds from toma-
toes with a teaspoon*

*Fill the tomatoes with the
ground meat mixture*

Cooked stuffed tomatoes are served hot on squares of toast (recipe is on page 41)

Croquettes, Rissoles and Kromeskis

Croquettes, rissoles and kromeskis are luxury ways of using cooked meat and poultry – they take more time but the finished dishes have no suggestion of 'leftover' about them. The following are entrée sizes to serve 4 people, but tiny versions make excellent hors d'oeuvre.

Croquettes are made with eggs, fish, veal or chicken that is finely chopped or ground and bound with a well-flavored thick sauce or panada. The mixture is chilled and rolled into cylinders, cork shapes or cones, coated with egg and breadcrumbs and fried in deep fat.

A good croquette has an even and golden brown crisp coating on the outside and a soft creamy center. To achieve this, the mixture should be made several hours ahead so it can be thoroughly chilled before shaping. If the mixture is very soft, a little gelatin may be added to help shaping – the gelatin has no setting effect on the croquette once it is heated in fat.

The deep fat must be at the right temperature – 375°F. If it is too cold the croquette will soften and the outer coating will be soggy; if it is too hot or the croquette is fried too long, the inside will burst through the coating.

Rissoles are made with cooked ground meat bound with gravy or brown sauce. The mixture should be firmer than for a croquette; it is wrapped in thinly rolled puff or pie pastry dough to form small turnovers and then fried in deep fat at a temperature of 350°F–365°F depending on the coating.

To make an extra crisp coating, rissoles wrapped in pie pastry dough may be brushed with egg, then rolled in crushed vermicelli pasta before frying.
Watchpoint: this cannot be done with puff pastry as the pastry puffs during cooking and the vermicelli coating falls off.

Kromeskis are savory fritters. The mixture is similar to that used for croquettes but it is rolled in bacon slices, dipped in batter and fried in deep fat at a temperature of 375°F.

Fried Parsley

Thoroughly wash and dry a small bunch of parsley and tie with a long string. After frying food allow fat to cool a little before lowering in parsley; stand back as it will spit. After 30 seconds or when spluttering stops, lift out parsley. Discard stems; drain sprigs on paper towels.

Chicken and Mushroom Croquettes

1½ cups cooked chicken, diced or chopped
2 cups (½ lb) mushrooms
salt and pepper
squeeze of lemon juice
1 envelope gelatin
¼ cup water
thick béchamel sauce, made with 3 tablespoons butter, 3 tablespoons flour and 1¼ cups milk (infused with slice of onion, 6 peppercorns, blade of mace and bay leaf)
1 egg yolk
deep fat (for frying)

For coating
1 egg, beaten to mix with ½ teaspoon olive oil
1 cup dry white breadcrumbs

For serving
hollandaise sauce or tomato sauce
fried parsley (for garnish)

Fat thermometer

Method
Put mushrooms in a buttered pan with 2–3 tablespoons water, seasoning and a squeeze of lemon juice. Cover and cook quickly for 2–3 minutes or until tender. Dice mushrooms reserving the liquid. Sprinkle gelatin over the ¼ cup water and let stand 5 minutes until spongy. Stir into béchamel sauce while it is still hot and add reserved mushroom liquid. Add diced chicken and mushrooms with egg yolk and season mixture well. Spread it 1–1½ inches thick in ice cube trays, cover and chill until very firm.

Cut mixture in even pieces and roll or pat on floured board into croquette shapes using 2 metal spatulas. When surface is smooth, brush with beaten egg and roll in breadcrumbs. This can be done 2–3 hours ahead and mixture refrigerated.

Heat deep fat to 375°F and dip empty frying basket into it – this will prevent croquettes from sticking. Lift out basket, place several croquettes in it, lower into hot fat and fry until golden brown. Drain on paper towels and keep warm while frying remaining croquettes. Serve with chosen sauce and garnish with fried parsley.

Tomato Sauce

Melt 2 tablespoons butter in a pan, stir in 1½ tablespoons flour and blend in 1½ cups stock or water, off the heat. Bring to a boil, stirring.

Cut 2 cups tomatoes (1 lb can, or 4 fresh tomatoes) in half and squeeze to remove seeds. (Peel fresh tomatoes only if you will be puréeing in a blender.) Strain the seeds to remove the juice. Add tomatoes and juice to the sauce with bouquet garni. Season, add a pinch of sugar and 1 teaspoon tomato paste to strengthen the flavor, if you like.

Cover the pan and simmer gently for 30 minutes or until the tomatoes are pulpy. Remove bouquet garni. Work the sauce through a strainer or purée in a blender. Return the sauce to the rinsed pan and adjust seasoning; simmer 5 minutes or until it is the right consistency.
Note: a tomato sauce should be of flowing, rather than coating consistency. For a good gloss, stir in 1 tablespoon butter before serving.

Creamy croquettes are coated with egg and breadcrumbs and fried in deep fat (recipe is on page 43)

Rissoles

1½ cup quantity rich pie pastry dough
1½ cups (½ lb) cooked beef, ground
1 small onion, finely chopped
1 tablespoon oil
salt and pepper
1–2 teaspoons Worcestershire sauce
2–3 tablespoons espagnole (see page 37) or tomato sauce (see page 43)
1 egg, beaten to mix with ½ teaspoon oil
½ cup crushed vermicelli pasta
deep fat (for frying)
espagnole sauce or tomato sauce – for serving

3–4 inch cookie cutter; fat thermometer

Method

Chill the pastry dough for 30 minutes. Fry onion in the oil until brown, add to the beef with seasoning and Worcestershire sauce to taste and add enough espagnole or tomato sauce to bind the mixture.

Roll out dough ¼ inch thick and cut out 3–4 inch rounds with a cookie cutter. Put 1 tablespoon filling in center of each round and brush edges with beaten egg. Fold over and pinch edges together to seal turnovers firmly. Brush them with beaten egg and roll in crushed vermicelli.

Heat deep fat to 350°F on a fat thermometer. Put several rissoles in a frying basket, lower them into the hot fat, increase temperature to 375°F and fry rissoles until golden brown. Drain them on paper towels and keep hot while frying remaining ones. Serve with espagnole or tomato sauce.

Rich Pie Pastry

For 2-cup quantity
2 cups flour
½ teaspoon salt
⅔ cup butter
1 egg yolk
3–4 tablespoons cold water

Method

Sift the flour with the salt into a bowl. Cut the butter into the flour until in small pieces and well coated, then rub in with the fingertips until the mixture looks like crumbs.

Make a well in the center and add the egg yolk and 3 tablespoons water and stir to combine. Draw the flour into the mixture in the center quickly with a knife. Press together with the fingers, adding more water if necessary to form a smooth dough.

Turn out the dough onto a floured board or marble slab and knead lightly for a few seconds until smooth. Wrap it in wax paper, plastic wrap or a plastic bag. Chill 30 minutes before using.

Chicken or Veal Kromeskis

2 cups cooked chicken or veal, chopped
thick béchamel sauce, made with 2 tablespoons butter, 2 tablespoons flour, ¾ cup milk (infused with slice of onion, 6 peppercorns, blade of mace and bay leaf)
salt and pepper
1 egg yolk
16–18 slices of bacon
deep fat (for frying)
tomato sauce (see page 43)

For fritter batter
1¼ cups flour
pinch of salt
½ package dry or ½ cake compressed yeast
1 cup lukewarm water
1 tablespoon oil

Fat thermometer

Method

To make the batter: sift flour and pinch of salt into a warm bowl. Sprinkle yeast over half the lukewarm water and let stand 5 minutes or until dissolved. Stir into the flour with the oil, then gradually beat in the remaining water to make a batter the consistency of thick cream. Beat well, cover and leave 15 minutes or until frothy.

Mix the chicken or veal with the béchamel sauce, season well, add the egg yolk and chill. Put 2 slices of bacon on a board so they overlap slightly lengthwise, put 1 tablespoon of mixture at one end and roll up. Shape the remaining kromeskis in the same way.

Heat the deep fat to 375°F on a fat thermometer. Dip the kromeskis, one at a time, into the batter, make sure they are completely coated and lower them with a slotted spoon into the hot fat. Fry them, a few at a time, until a deep golden brown, then lift out and drain on paper towels. Keep hot while coating and frying the remaining kromeskis. Serve hot with tomato sauce.

Shrimp Kromeskis

1 cup (⅓ lb) cooked peeled, shrimps, chopped
thick béchamel sauce, made with 3 tablespoons butter, 3 tablespoons flour, 1¼ cups milk (infused with blade of mace, slice of onion, bay leaf, 6 peppercorns)
1 cup (⅓ lb) mushrooms
squeeze lemon juice
salt
black pepper, freshly ground
2 egg yolks
16–18 strips bacon
fritter batter (see chicken or veal kromeskis)
tomato sauce (for serving)

Method

Make the béchamel sauce. Put the mushrooms in a pan with 1–2 tablespoons water and a squeeze of lemon juice. Cover and cook over high heat 1–2 minutes until just tender. Drain, reserving the liquid, and dice them. Add the mushrooms and liquid to the béchamel sauce with the chopped shrimps, taste for seasoning, add the egg yolks and chill.

Prepare and fry the kromeskis as for chicken or veal kromeskis. Serve hot with tomato sauce.

Serve the pork tenderloin cut in slices to show the prune and almond stuffing (recipe is on page 51)

Serve cream of cheese soup as an overture to the sweet and sour flavors of pork stuffed with prunes and the melting richness of coffee meringue cake or orange macaroon syllabub.

A white wine on the sweet side is usually welcome with pork. This is particularly true in this recipe where the roast's natural sweetness is increased by the prune stuffing. An appropriate accompaniment would be a Vouvray white — of the Demi-sec (half dry) variety — from France's Loire Valley. For a fuller, more 'grapey' bouquet and flavor, you might try one of the traditional white wines like a Delaware, from New York's Finger Lakes region.

Potage Crème de Fromage
(Cream of Cheese Soup)

Cheese Puffs

Pork Tenderloin with Prunes
Julienne of Celery & Potato

Coffee Meringue Cake
or
Orange Macaroon Syllabub

∿

White wine — Vouvray Demi-sec (Loire)
or Delaware (New York)

PORK WITH PRUNES STRIKES A SWEET NOTE

TIMETABLE

Day before
Make meringue layers and coffee butter cream frosting. Fill and finish the cake, arrange on serving dish, cover and store in refrigerator.
Soak prunes overnight in freshly brewed tea.

Morning
Prepare soup but do not add liaison or cheese.
Make and bake cheese puffs.
Prepare, stuff and tie pork tenderloins.
Cook remaining prunes in wine and set aside in pan.
Cook onions, drain and cover.
Cut potatoes and celery in julienne strips, keep potatoes in a bowl of cold water; wrap celery in plastic wrap.
Make orange macaroon syllabub and keep, covered, in the refrigerator.

Assemble ingredients for final cooking from 7 p.m. for dinner around 8 p.m.

Order of Work

7:00
Brown tied pork tenderloin and leave to cook.

7:40
Cook julienne of celery and potato and keep warm.

7:45
Transfer pork to serving platter, slice and keep warm; make sauce. Heat onion and prune garnish; keep warm.
Put soup on to heat, but do not boil.

8:00
Add liaison and cheese to soup and serve.

You will find that **cooking times** given in the individual recipes for these dishes have sometimes been adapted in the timetable to help you when cooking and serving this menu as a party meal.

Appetizer

Potage Crème de Fromage
(Cream of Cheese Soup)

1 Bermuda or large onion, finely chopped
2 tablespoons butter
$\frac{1}{4}$ cup flour
4 cups milk (infused with slice of onion, 6 peppercorns, blade of mace and bay leaf)
salt and pepper
pinch of cayenne or dash of Tabasco
2 egg yolks (for liaison)
$\frac{1}{4}$ cup heavy cream (for liaison)
$\frac{1}{2}$ cup grated Cheddar cheese

For garnish
2–3 tablespoons cooked green peas
cheese puffs

Method
Blanch the chopped onion by putting it in a pan with cold water and bringing to a boil. Drain, refresh and drain again.

Melt the butter in a saucepan, add the onion, cover and cook over a low heat for 5 minutes or until the onion is very soft, but not browned. Remove from the heat and stir in the flour. Strain in the infused milk, salt, pepper and cayenne or Tabasco, and bring to a boil, stirring. Simmer over a low heat for 6–7 minutes. Strain and return to the pan.

To make the liaison: mix egg yolks in a bowl with the cream and stir in a little hot soup. Stir this mixture into remaining soup, with the grated cheese. Reheat carefully over a low heat, stirring constantly, until soup is hot; do not let it boil. Stir in peas; serve soup with cheese puffs.

Cheese Puffs

Make a small quantity of choux pastry in the following proportions (be sure to measure accurately): $\frac{1}{2}$ cup flour, pinch of salt, $\frac{1}{2}$ cup water, $\frac{1}{4}$ cup butter and 2 eggs. Stir in $\frac{1}{4}$ cup grated Parmesan cheese.

Spoon dough into a pastry bag fitted with a $\frac{1}{4}$ inch plain tube and pipe tiny mounds on a dampened baking sheet. Brush with egg glaze and bake in a hot oven (400°F) for 12–15 minutes or until the puffs are brown and crisp. Cool before serving.

A sweet note

Serve potage crème de fromage garnished with cooked green peas and cheese puffs

Slit both tenderloins and open up; stuff the prunes

Lay six stuffed prunes on one tenderloin

Place second tenderloin on top to cover prunes

Tie tenderloins together with string in a neat roll

50

Entrée

Pork Tenderloin with Prunes

2 pork tenderloins (about 1 lb each)
18 large prunes
6 anchovy fillets, soaked in a little milk
6 whole, blanched almonds
3 tablespoons butter
2 teaspoons flour
1½ cups well-flavored stock
salt and pepper
1 cup red wine
12 small onions, blanched and peeled
1 teaspoon arrowroot (mixed to a paste with 1 tablespoon stock or water) – optional

Method

Soak the prunes overnight in freshly brewed tea, then remove the pits.

Make a slit down the length of each tenderloin and open the meat so it is flat. Stuff 6 prunes with a drained anchovy fillet wrapped around a blanched almond and lay them on one tenderloin. Cover this with the second opened tenderloin and tie them together neatly with string.

Brown the pork all over in a skillet or shallow flameproof casserole in the butter. Sprinkle in the flour and cook for 2–3 minutes until brown. Pour in the stock, stir until smooth and bring to a boil. Season, cover pan and simmer gently for 40–50 minutes or until pork is tender.

Simmer remaining prunes, uncovered, in wine for 10–15 minutes or until tender and most of the wine has evaporated.

Boil the onions in salted water to cover for 12–15 minutes or until tender. Drain and keep hot.

Transfer pork to a hot platter, remove string and carve meat in three-eighth inch slices. Pour wine from prunes into meat pan, bring to a boil and, if you want to thicken the sauce, stir in the arrowroot paste and heat just until sauce thickens. Adjust seasoning and spoon sauce over the meat. Garnish platter with the prunes and onions, mixed together.

Serve with a julienne mixture of celery and potato.

Accompaniment to entrée

Julienne of Celery and Potato

bunch of celery
3 medium potatoes
2 tablespoons butter
1 shallot, finely chopped
salt
black pepper, freshly ground
1 tablespoon chopped parsley (for garnish)

Method

Trim the celery and peel the potatoes and cut them into julienne strips about 1½–2 inches long and one-eighth inch thick. Keep the potatoes in a bowl of cold water until needed.

Heat the butter in a skillet or flameproof casserole, add the celery and shallot, cover and cook for 4–5 minutes, shaking the pan to prevent sticking. The vegetables should not brown. This cooking can be done in advance.

Drain the potatoes and pat them dry with paper towels. Add them to the pan and season. Stir the vegetable mixture together carefully, cover with foil and a lid and cook 8–10 minutes on top of the stove or in a moderate oven (350°F) until the potatoes are just tender.

Sprinkle with chopped parsley and serve in a vegetable dish.

Note: if this dish is prepared and cooked without interruption and a shallow pan is used on top of the stove, as above, the potatoes will take about 8–10 minutes; they should not be cooked in advance. However, if celery and shallot are cooked in advance, vegetables will take 10–12 minutes on top of stove or 15–20 minutes in oven to reheat and finish cooking.

Keep julienne potatoes in cold water until needed. Trim the celery and cut into julienne strips. Chop shallot and parsley

Coffee Meringue Cake

4 egg whites
1 cup sugar
1½ cup quantity coffee butter
    cream frosting

For decoration
¾ cup whole blanched almonds,
    browned and finely chopped
confectioners' sugar (for
    sprinkling)

Method

Line 3 baking sheets with silicone paper and draw an 8–9 inch circle on each one. Set oven at very low (275°F).

To make meringue: beat egg whites in a bowl until they hold a stiff peak, add 4 teaspoons of the measured sugar and continue beating for about 30 seconds until the mixture is glossy. Gradually fold in the remaining sugar with a large metal spoon.

Divide meringue evenly among the 3 baking sheets and spread into circles.

Bake meringues in heated oven for 50–60 minutes or until dry and crisp. Let circles cool but peel off the paper before the meringues are completely cold.

Make the coffee butter cream frosting.

When the rounds of meringue are cold, spread them with some of the coffee butter cream frosting and sandwich the layers together. Spread the top and sides with remaining butter cream and cover with finely chopped almonds.

Cut 4 strips of wax paper about 1 inch wide and lay them across top of cake, parallel to each other, leaving about 1 inch between strips. Generously sprinkle top of

cake with confectioners' sugar, then carefully lift off each strip of paper.

For butter cream frosting pour hot syrup into egg yolks and beat until thick and light

When meringue is cold, sandwich layers and spread top and sides with frosting

Coffee Butter Cream Frosting

½ cup sugar
5 tablespoons water
4 egg yolks
1½ cups unsalted butter
2–3 tablespoons dry
    instant coffee (dissolved
    in 1 tablespoon hot
    water)

Method

Dissolve the sugar in the water over a low heat, then boil steadily until it forms a thin thread when tested between thumb and forefinger (230°F–234°F on a sugar thermometer).

While syrup is still hot pour it into egg yolks, beating hard; continue beating until mixture is cool, thick and light. In a separate bowl cream butter until soft and beat in egg and sugar mixture a little at a time. Add enough coffee to give a good flavor.

Orange Macaroon Syllabub

grated rind and juice of 1 orange
3–4 tablespoons Grand
    Marnier, Curaçao, Triple
    Sec or other orange liqueur
4 large macaroons, crumbled
4–6 tablespoons sugar
½ cup Sauternes or sweet
    white wine
1½ cups heavy cream

4 parfait or stemmed glasses

Method

Sprinkle the orange liqueur over the macaroons and leave to soak.

Mix together the orange juice, sugar and wine and stir until the sugar is dissolved; add the grated orange rind.

Whip the cream until it holds a soft shape, then gradually add the wine mixture, whisking until the cream again holds a soft shape.

Spoon a little of the orange syllabub into the glasses, add a layer of macaroon crumbs and continue adding layers of syllabub and crumbs until all are used, ending with syllabub. Cover and chill 3–4 hours before serving.

Coffee meringue cake is covered with finely chopped almonds and sprinkled with bands of confectioners' sugar

Tuna and shrimp salad (recipe is on page 57)

ANTIPASTO APPETIZERS

Here, salad to start a meal comes as no surprise. Anything from a simple green salad to an avocado filled with crab meat may be offered as an appetizer. Italians go one step further in their 'antipasti', with a varied selection that usually includes prosciutto, salami, olives and perhaps tomatoes or marinated mushrooms.

There is almost no limit to the choice of recipes — in fact, the greater the variety, the better the antipasto. The number of kinds of antipasto you serve depends on the number of guests, but in general there should be two or three simple dishes like sliced salami, garlic or liver sausage, pickled herring or fillets of anchovy, together with two or three salads, flavored with a variety of dressings. If you have a good selection, guests can start with fish, then go on to meat and vegetable dishes — like a meal in miniature.

The traditional antipasto dish is rectangular, about $2\frac{1}{2}$ inches deep and usually made of white china, or you can use any convenient matching dishes. Special antipasto trays are available with compartments or dishes that interlock. Antipasti can also be arranged in scallop shells — put two or three kinds in one shell and serve a shell for each person. For a small party or when time is short, this method of serving is often easier than having a large selection of different dishes.

If you serve antipasto or salads regularly, it is worth making a large quantity of mayonnaise and vinaigrette dressing and storing them in airtight jars in a cool place. When you keep mayonnaise in the refrigerator, be sure to bring it to room temperature before using; if it gets too cold and separates, add 1—2 tablespoons of boiling water and whisk well.

Attractive garnishes are essential to good antipasti and a colorful touch of lemon or sliced tomato can make all the difference. Arrange mixtures neatly in the dishes and place the dishes so that antipasto of contrasting colors are aligned.

Many of the following choice of antipasto dishes can be served alone as an appetizer or as part of a selection for a buffet lunch.

Sliced peppers and tomatoes add color to frankfurter and ham salad

Anchovy and bean salad is decorated with anchovies

Frankfurter and Ham Salad

2–3 frankfurters
½ cup (¼ lb) cooked ham, cut in
    strips
1 tomato, peeled, seeded and
    cut in strips
1 red or green pepper, cored,
    seeded, cut in strips and
    blanched

For dressing
1 tablespoon white wine
    vinegar
1 teaspoon tomato paste
3 tablespoons oil
½ teaspoon sugar (or to taste)
salt and pepper

Method
Cook frankfurters in simmering water for 5–6 minutes, drain and cool them. Slice diagonally and mix with the ham, tomato and pepper strips.

Whisk together ingredients for dressing, season to taste, pour over frankfurter mixture, toss with a fork and pile in a serving dish.

Tuna and Shrimp Salad

small can (3¼ oz) tuna in
    oil, drained
¼ lb cooked, peeled small
    shrimps
5–6 stalks of celery
⅓ cup vinaigrette dressing
    (made with lemon juice
    instead of vinegar) –
    see page 61
1 tablespoon chopped parsley

Method
Cut celery into 1½ inch thin sticks and soak them in ice water for 30 minutes until crisp. Drain and dry on paper towels.

Flake tuna with a fork and mix with shrimps and celery. Spoon over vinaigrette dressing, add chopped parsley and arrange in a serving dish.

Tomato Salad with Lemon Dressing

2 large ripe tomatoes, peeled
    and sliced

For lemon dressing
peeled rind of ½ lemon
1 tablespoon lemon juice
2 tablespoons oil
2 tablespoons light cream
½ teaspoon salt
1½ teaspoons sugar
black pepper, freshly ground

Method
Peel and slice tomatoes and arrange them, overlapping, in a serving dish.

To make the lemon dressing: beat all the ingredients except the lemon rind together and taste for seasoning. Spoon the lemon dressing over the tomatoes.

Cut lemon rind into fine shreds, blanch 5 minutes in boiling water, drain and dry on paper towels. Sprinkle over tomato salad.

Quantities
Any two of these recipes will serve four people as an appetizer or three people as an entrée.

Anchovy and Bean Salad

small can anchovy fillets
1½ cups cooked fava beans,
    drained

For dressing
½ teaspoon grated onion
2 teaspoons white wine
    vinegar
2 tablespoons oil
1 teaspoon anchovy paste
2 tablespoons heavy cream
1 tablespoon chopped parsley

Method
Whisk together all ingredients for the dressing, mix it with beans and arrange in a serving dish. Split anchovy fillets in half lengthwise and arrange in a lattice over beans.

To Cook Dried Fava Beans
Wash beans unless package states otherwise and pick over to remove any grit. Soak beans in 3–4 times their volume of lukewarm water for 8 hours or overnight. Discard any beans that float. If beans have to be left longer, change the water or they may start to ferment.

Drain beans, cover with fresh warm water, add lid and simmer for about 1–1½ hours or until tender. Do not add salt until halfway through cooking to avoid toughening skins.

Drain cooked beans and use as specified in recipe.

Corn, pimiento and pickled onions are a popular salad mixture

Corn, Pimiento and Pickled Onion Salad

1½ cups cooked corn kernels
2 slices of canned pimiento, drained and coarsely chopped
4–6 small pickled onions, quartered or thinly sliced
salt and pepper
¼ cup vinaigrette dressing (see page 61) or lemon dressing (see tomato salad – on page 57)

Method
Mix corn with pimiento and pickled onions and season well. Moisten with vinaigrette or lemon dressing and arrange in a serving dish.

Rice, Tomato and Ripe Olive Salad

⅓ cup rice
2 medium tomatoes, peeled, seeded and cut in strips
⅓ cup ripe olives, halved and pitted
1 cup (¼ lb) mushrooms
¼ cup water
juice of ½ lemon
3–4 tablespoons vinaigrette dressing (made with white wine instead of vinegar) – see page 61
salt and pepper

Method
Cook rice in boiling salted water for 10–12 minutes or until just tender, drain, refresh, drain again and spread out to dry. Trim mushrooms so stalks are level with caps, quarter and cook quickly with water and lemon juice for 2–3 minutes, so that liquid is well reduced; shake pan occasionally during cooking.

Mix rice, half the tomato strips, olives and mushrooms (reserving 5–6 of each), add dressing, season and stir. Pile in serving dish. Decorate with remaining tomato strips, olives and mushrooms.

Herring and Dill Pickle Salad

1 jar (8 oz) herring in wine sauce
2 large dill pickles, sliced
1 Bermuda or other mild onion, sliced
3–4 tablespoons vinaigrette dressing (made with white wine instead of vinegar) – see page 61

Method
Push onion slices into rings and blanch them in boiling water for 5–6 minutes. Drain, refresh and dry on paper towels.

Arrange pickle slices around the edge of a serving dish. Mix herring pieces with onion rings and pile in the center of the dish. Spoon over the vinaigrette dressing and chill.

Quantities
Any two of these recipes will serve four people as an appetizer or three people as an entrée.

Herring and dill pickle salad is flavored with onion rings

Italian salad is made with pasta shells, ham and olives

Note: for an even simpler herring salad, drain the herring pieces and top them with grated fresh horseradish or mix 1–2 tablespoons prepared horseradish with $\frac{1}{2}$ cup cream, whipped until it holds a soft shape, and spoon over the herring.

Egg Mayonnaise

2–3 hard-cooked eggs
$\frac{2}{3}$ cup mayonnaise (made with lemon juice instead of vinegar) – see page 11
1 tablespoon coarsely chopped parsley
$\frac{1}{4}$ cup cooked, peeled, chopped shrimps (optional)

A curry-flavored mayonnaise like that used for curried potato salad is also good with hard-cooked eggs.

Method
Cut eggs in half lengthwise and arrange them in a serving dish, rounded side up. Thin mayonnaise to a coating consistency with water. Coat eggs with mayonnaise and sprinkle generously with chopped parsley. If you like, scatter chopped shrimps over the eggs before coating them with mayonnaise.

Watchpoint: when coating eggs with mayonnaise, make sure eggs are quite dry, otherwise it will slide off the smooth whites.

Italian Salad

$\frac{1}{2}$ cup conchiglie (pasta shells)
$\frac{1}{2}$ cup ($\frac{1}{4}$ lb) cooked ham, cut in strips
$\frac{1}{3}$ cup ripe olives, halved and pitted
1 teaspoon Dijon-style mustard
$\frac{1}{4}$ cup mayonnaise (see page 11)

Method
Simmer conchiglie in boiling salted water until only just tender (time depends on their size so follow cooking instructions on package). Drain, refresh and well drain again.

Add conchiglie to ham and olives. Stir mustard into mayonnaise, combine with pasta mixture and arrange in a serving dish.

Curried Potato Salad

6–8 small new potatoes, unpeeled
2–3 tablespoons vinaigrette dressing
⅓ cup mayonnaise (see page 11)

For curry mixture
1 tablespoon curry powder
2 tablespoons olive oil
1 shallot or small onion, sliced
1 teaspoon paprika
½ cup tomato juice
slice of lemon
2 teaspoons apricot jam or red currant jelly

Method
To make curry mixture: heat oil and cook shallot or onion until soft. Stir in curry powder and paprika, cook over low heat for 1 minute and add tomato juice, lemon and jam or jelly. Cover and simmer 7–10 minutes; strain. Keep mixture in a covered container in refrigerator for up to 1 week or until needed.

Cook the potatoes in boiling salted water until just tender, drain them, peel while still hot, mix with vinaigrette dressing and let cool. Mix enough curry mixture with mayonnaise to flavor it to taste. Put potatoes in a serving dish and coat with curry mayonnaise.

Salmon Muscovite

¼ lb finely sliced smoked salmon
1 jar (2 oz) red or black caviar
2 hard-cooked eggs
1 lemon, cut into wedges

Method
Cut eggs in half, scoop out yolks and work them through a sieve; chop the whites. Shape the smoked salmon into small cones, spoon a little caviar into each and arrange the cones in a circle on a serving dish. Place small mounds of egg yolk and egg white at alternate corners of the dish and garnish with lemon wedges. Chill thoroughly before serving.

Cucumber Salad

Peel 1 large or 2 small cucumbers and slice thinly. Sprinkle lightly with salt, press slices well between 2 plates and leave in a cool place for 1 hour to draw out the juices (dégorger). Drain and rinse with cold water and pat dry. Arrange slices in a serving dish and spoon over 3–4 tablespoons vinaigrette dressing, plain yogurt or sour cream. Sprinkle with 1 tablespoon chopped chives and serve chilled.

Marinated Oysters

½ pint shucked select oysters, with their liquor
¼ cup white wine
¼ cup oil
juice of ½ lemon
2 teaspoons chopped parsley
1 teaspoon chopped chives

Method
Mix together wine, oil, lemon juice and herbs and pour over the oysters in a pan. Bring just to a boil, transfer to a serving dish and chill.

Vegetable Salad

1 medium carrot, diced
1 medium potato, diced
¼ cup cooked peas
1 cup cooked diced beets
2–3 tablespoons vinaigrette dressing
⅓ cup mayonnaise (see page 11)

Method
Cook carrot in boiling salted water for 10–12 minutes or until just tender; drain. Cook potato in boiling salted water for 5–6 minutes or until just tender; drain. Mix all vegetables together and moisten with vinaigrette dressing. Leave until cold, then stir in the mayonnaise.

Watchpoint: the amount of carrot, potato and peas combined should be half that of the beets.

Spiced Onions

10–12 (¾ lb) small white onions, peeled and blanched
2 medium tomatoes, peeled, seeded and coarsely chopped
1 cup white wine
3 tablespoons olive oil
1 teaspoon chopped fresh fennel, or ½ teaspoon fennel seeds
1 teaspoon coriander seeds
salt and pepper

Method
Combine all ingredients in a pan with seasoning, cover and simmer gently for 35–40 minutes; the onions should be very tender but still whole. Carefully transfer onions to a serving dish and strain over the cooking liquid. Serve very cold.

To Prepare Artichoke Bottoms

Cut the stalks from large artichokes and pull away the lower leaves. Cut the tops off remaining leaves, leaving about 1 inch at the base. Cook artichokes in boiling salted water for 20–25 minutes or until tender, drain and cool slightly.

Pull away the remaining leaves and scoop out the hairy chokes with a teaspoon. Use artichoke bottoms as attractive containers for garnishes of cooked peas or mushrooms or as a base for salads.

Cucumber salad is sprinkled with chopped chives

Artichokes Niçoise

4 cooked artichoke bottoms
3 tablespoons vinaigrette
   dressing (made with lemon
   juice instead of vinegar)
1 tablespoon chopped parsley
   (for garnish)

For tomato fondue
2 ripe tomatoes, peeled,
   seeded and chopped, or
   1½ cups (¾ lb) canned
   Italian-type plum tomatoes,
   drained and crushed
2 tablespoons olive oil
2 shallots, finely chopped
1 clove of garlic, crushed
bouquet garni
salt and pepper

Method
Spoon vinaigrette dressing
over the artichoke bottoms
and let stand to marinate for
30 minutes.

   To make tomato fondue: in
a skillet heat oil and fry shallot until soft. Add tomatoes,
garlic, bouquet garni and
seasoning and cook, stirring,
until mixture is rich and thick.
Remove bouquet garni and
cool.

   Pile tomato fondue on artichoke bottoms, arrange in a
serving dish and sprinkle with
chopped parsley.

Tomato fondue, literally
melted tomato, is a con-
centrated mixture of tomatoes which have been
cooked in butter or oil until
thick. It is often flavored
with onion and garlic and
is used to flavor or garnish
egg, meat, poultry and fish
dishes.

Vinaigrette Dressing
For every tablespoon vinegar (red or white wine,
cider or tarragon) use 3
tablespoons oil (preferably
olive or peanut). Mix vinegar with ¼ teaspoon salt,
¼ teaspoon freshly ground
pepper, and chopped fresh
herbs (thyme, marjoram,
basil or parsley) to taste.
Gradually add oil, whisk-
ing until dressing thickens
slightly. Taste for seasoning.

Tuna and shrimp salad is one ▶
of many simple to make anti-
pasto dishes (recipe is on
page 57)

Brains Bourguignon, garnished with a bacon, onion and mushroom mixture, are served on croûtes (recipe is on page 64)

VARIETY MEATS (2)

Brains and sweetbreads are luxury variety meats — sought after by gourmets and the basis of many distinctive dishes: however they have never been generally popular. One reason for this unpopularity is that sweetbreads and brains are often poorly prepared. To be at their best they must be very fresh and they must be carefully blanched and cleaned to remove all membrane before cooking. Do not freeze brains or sweetbreads as this tends to spoil their delicate flavor and texture.

Tongue is another variety meat that lends itself to a wide range of excellent dishes. Smoked tongues are readily available and fresh tongues can be found at most butchers — both kinds are an excellent buy as they are relatively inexpensive and quality is reliable.

Liver, kidneys and other variety meats were discussed in Volume 9.

BRAINS

Brains must be very fresh and firm with a bright color — calves' and sheep's brains are the best, though pigs' brains are also available. They come in pairs and a set of sheep's or small calves' brains serves 2 people; larger sets of calves' brains will serve 3–4 people.

To prepare brains: soak them thoroughly in well-salted water for 2–3 hours, changing the water once or twice. Wash them thoroughly in warm water to remove all traces of blood, then blanch them by putting in cold water with 1 tablespoon vinegar, bringing to a boil and draining them. Rinse them and trim away any skin or membrane.

To poach brains: brains are always partly cooked in court bouillon (see box on opposite page) before the final cooking. Lower the brains with a slotted spoon into simmering court bouillon (there should be just enough liquid to cover them) and poach in the liquid (i.e. at just below boiling point) for 15–20 minutes or until quite firm to the touch. Drain them.

Cooking can be completed in a variety of ways — for example the brains can be sautéed, or served with a wine or butter sauce as in the following recipes.

Cervelles au Beurre Noir
(Brains with Black Butter)

2 sets of small calves' or sheep's brains
4 cups court bouillon (see box)

For black butter
6 tablespoons butter
salt
black pepper, freshly ground
3 tablespoons capers
2 tablespoons wine vinegar
1 tablespoon chopped parsley

For serving
1 lemon, cut in wedges
10–12 small new potatoes, boiled or steamed

This is the simplest and most famous way of serving brains. The piquant capers and vinegar in the black butter are an ideal foil for the creamy texture and slightly bland flavor of brains.

Method

Soak and blanch brains, then poach them in court bouillon until just firm. Drain them well on paper towels, arrange in a hot serving dish and keep warm.

To make black butter: in a skillet or frying pan heat the butter with a little salt and pepper, and cook to a rich brown (not black) color. At once add capers, vinegar and parsley and spoon the mixture, while foaming, over the brains.

Garnish the dish with lemon wedges and boiled small new potatoes and serve at once.

> A recipe for curried brains is given on page 86.

Brains Bourguignon

2 sets of calves' brains
4 cups court bouillon (see box)
5 rounds of bread, about 2½ inches in diameter (for croûtes)
3–4 tablespoons oil and butter, mixed (for frying croûtes)

For wine sauce
1 cup red Burgundy
1 tablespoon butter
1 medium onion, finely chopped
2 teaspoons flour
½ cup well-flavored beef stock
salt and pepper
½ tablespoon butter (to finish)

For garnish
12–16 small onions, peeled
¼ lb piece of bacon
1 tablespoon butter
1 cup (¼ lb) mushrooms, sliced
1 tablespoon chopped parsley

This recipe can also be used for sweetbreads. The sauce can be made a day ahead if you like.

Method

Soak and blanch brains, then poach them in court bouillon until just firm. Drain them well on paper towels and keep warm.

To make sauce: boil wine until reduced by about one-eighth. In a frying pan heat butter and fry onion until lightly browned, stir in the flour and, after a few seconds, add the reduced wine and stock. Bring to a boil, stirring, and simmer 5–6 minutes until the sauce is glossy and slightly thickened; taste for seasoning and reserve.

Fry croûtes in oil and butter until golden brown on both sides, drain and arrange on a warm platter. Wipe out pan.

To prepare garnish: blanch the small onions, drain them, then cook in boiling salted water for 10–15 minutes or until just tender. Drain them and reserve.

Cut bacon into lardons (strips about ¼ inch square and 1 inch long), blanch them for 2 minutes and drain. Melt 1 tablespoon butter in the frying pan, add lardons and fry until beginning to brown. Add mushrooms and, after 30 seconds, the reserved onions. Cook, shaking the pan to prevent sticking, until the mushrooms are tender and onions are heated.

To serve: arrange brains on top of the croûtes. Heat the sauce, stir in the ½ tablespoon butter off the heat and spoon over the brains. Sprinkle with chopped parsley and garnish the platter with the bacon, mushroom and onion mixture.

Poach brains in court bouillon for brains Bourguignon

Add the cooked onions to bacon lardons and mushrooms to make the garnish

Court Bouillon

For 4 cup quantity, combine 4 cups water, 1 sliced carrot, 1 small onion (quartered and stuck with a clove), bouquet garni, 6 peppercorns and 2 tablespoons white distilled vinegar, white wine vinegar or lemon juice in a pan with a little salt. Cover, bring to a boil and simmer 15–20 minutes. Strain and use.

Fritot of Brains

2 sets of calves' brains
4 cups court bouillon
4–5 tablespoons butter (preferably clarified) – for frying
2 tablespoons butter (unclarified)
1 lemon
salt and pepper

For coating
¼ cup seasoned flour (made with ¼ teaspoon salt, pinch of pepper)
1 egg, beaten to mix
½ cup dry white breadcrumbs

Method

Soak and blanch brains, then poach them in court bouillon until just firm. Drain them well on paper towels and leave until cold. Roll them lightly in seasoned flour, brush them with beaten egg and coat with the breadcrumbs.

In a skillet or frying pan heat clarified butter and fry brains over medium heat,

turning them and basting frequently, until golden brown. Transfer them to a warm serving dish.

Wipe out the pan, melt the unclarified butter and, when a nut-brown (noisette) color, add the juice of half the lemon with seasoning. Pour noisette butter at once, while still foaming, over the brains. Serve the brains very hot with the remaining half of lemon, cut into wedges.

A **fritot** is a kind of fritter made with small pieces of meat, poultry or variety meats and is a popular way of serving brains. A fritot can be served with a sharp sauce such as the tartare sauce in fritot of sweetbreads (see page 67) or, a little noisette butter can be poured over just before serving as for fritot of brains.

SWEETBREADS

The most sought-after of all variety meats, sweetbreads are prized for their delicate flavor and a smooth, creamy texture that is never soft like that of brains. They are a gland found near the heart and throat of young animals.

Calves' sweetbreads are the only ones generally available – good ones from milk-fed calves are compact and white with no traces of pink (pinkness indicates the animal was not milk fed). Calves' sweetbreads are

sold by the pair and 2–3 pairs (1½ lb) are enough for 4 people.

Lambs' sweetbreads can sometimes be found. They are smaller than calves' sweetbreads and they too are white and tender. They are usually used for filling vol-au-vents or bouchées or for a ragoût when small pieces of meat are needed. Baby beef sweetbreads are also sold; they are redder in color than calves' and lambs' and can be tough; 1½ lb lamb or beef sweetbreads are enough for 4 people and they should be prepared in the same way as calves' sweetbreads.

To prepare sweetbreads: soak them for 3–5 hours in cold salted water to which 1–2 slices of lemon or a few drops of vinegar have been added. Rinse them and put in a pan with water to cover. Add a little salt and another slice of lemon and bring to a boil over low heat, skimming the top from time to time. Drain sweetbreads and rinse them quickly in cold water. Remove any ducts and skin that will pull off easily. Press sweetbreads until cold between 2 flat plates with a 2 lb weight on top – this makes them firm and easy to slice. They are now ready to be braised, sautéed or fried.

Calves' sweetbreads are suggested for all the recipes on these pages because they are the best and are generally available. However **lamb** or **beef sweetbreads** can be substituted in sweetbread recipes for fritot, fricandeau, bonne maman, and soubise.

Sauté of Sweetbreads with White Wine Sauce

2–3 pairs (1½ lb) calves' sweetbreads
½ cup white wine
3–4 tablespoons butter
2 shallots, finely chopped
1 cup (¼ lb) mushrooms, thinly sliced
1 teaspoon flour
1 cup well-flavored veal stock
1–2 tablespoons heavy cream (optional)
salt and pepper

For garnish
1 lb green beans
2 tablespoons butter

Method

Soak, blanch and trim the sweetbreads and press them between 2 plates until cold.

In a skillet or frying pan, heat the butter and brown sweetbreads on all sides over medium heat. Take them out, add shallot and cook until soft. Add the wine, boil to reduce it to a little more than half, then add mushrooms. Cook 1 minute or until tender, take from heat and sprinkle over flour. Pour in the stock, bring to a boil, stirring, then put back sweetbreads and add salt and pepper to taste. Cover and simmer gently for 25–35 minutes until sweetbreads are very tender.

Slice sweetbreads and arrange in a warm serving dish. Add the cream, if used, to the sauce, taste for seasoning and spoon over the sweetbreads. Garnish the dish with green beans, cooked in boiling salted water for 15–18 minutes or until tender, then drained thoroughly and tossed in butter. If you like, serve mashed potatoes separately.

Fricandeau of Sweetbreads

2–3 pairs (1½ lb) calves'
  sweetbreads
3 tablespoons butter
1 cup red wine
1 large carrot, sliced
1 large onion, sliced
5–6 stalks of celery, sliced
bouquet garni
1 cup well-flavored stock
kneaded butter (made with
  2 tablespoons butter,
  1 tablespoon flour)
salt and pepper

Method
Soak, blanch and trim sweetbreads and press them between 2 plates until cold.

In a shallow flameproof casserole heat the butter and brown sweetbreads on all sides over medium heat. Remove them, add the wine and boil to reduce it to a little less than half. Add vegetables, cover and simmer gently for 5–6 minutes. Put sweetbreads on top, add bouquet garni and stock, cover and braise in a moderate oven (350°F) for 35–45 minutes or until sweetbreads are very tender.

Remove sweetbreads from casserole, slice them and arrange in a warm serving dish. Strain the sauce, boil to reduce it a little and thicken by whisking in the kneaded butter a little at a time. Simmer 2 minutes, taste for seasoning and spoon over sweetbreads.

Serve with boiled or steamed small new potatoes.

Sweetbreads Tante Marie

2–3 pairs of sweetbreads
1 cup veal or chicken stock
3 tablespoons oil
scant ½ cup butter
2 medium onions, quartered
2 cloves of garlic, split in half
salt and pepper
1 teaspoon flour
2 tablespoons brandy
¾ cup dry white wine
bouquet garni
2 cups (½ lb) small mushrooms
4–5 croûtes of bread
1 tablespoon tomato purée
a little kneaded butter (made
  with 2 tablespoons butter
  and 1 tablespoon flour)
½ cup heavy cream

Method
Prepare sweetbreads. Simmer them in the stock for 10 minutes, drain well and pat dry with paper towels. Reserve the stock in which they were cooked.

Heat oil and 3 tablespoons butter in a skillet, add onions and garlic, salt and pepper and cook over a fairly high heat, stirring frequently, for 2–3 minutes. Add sweetbreads and brown them, turning frequently. Sprinkle with flour; when well mixed, add brandy, heat it and flame. Add wine, reserved stock and bouquet garni. Bring to a boil, cover and simmer 40 minutes or until sweetbreads are very tender.

Trim mushroom stems level with bases of caps and sauté caps in 1 tablespoon butter. Set aside. Brown croûtes in remaining butter and arrange them in an ovenproof dish. Slice sweetbreads in half and place on the croûtes. Strain liquid from pan into a clean pan and stir tomato purée into it, then add kneaded butter and cream. Bring this sauce to a boil, stirring, and add seasoning. Spoon over the sweetbreads and surround them with the mushrooms. Serve with green beans and small new potatoes tossed in butter and parsley.

Sweetbreads with chestnuts surrounded by the ingredients

Sweetbreads with Chestnuts

2–3 pairs (1½ lb) calves'
  sweetbreads
2 tablespoons butter
2 shallots, finely chopped
8–10 large pitted prunes
½ cup red wine
2 teaspoons flour
2 cups well-flavored stock
salt and pepper
bouquet garni

For garnish
1 lb chestnuts
12–16 small onions
2 tablespoons butter
1 teaspoon sugar
1 cup stock
2–3 slices of bread, crusts
  removed, cut in triangles and
  fried in 3–4 tablespoons oil
  and butter, mixed (for
  croûtes)

Method
Soak, blanch and trim sweet-breads and press them between 2 plates until cold.

In a shallow flameproof casserole heat the butter and brown sweetbreads on all sides. Remove them, add shallot and prunes and cook 1–2 minutes until shallot is soft. Add the wine, bring to a boil and flame. Simmer until wine is reduced by about one-quarter, then stir in flour. Pour on stock, bring to a boil, and add seasoning and bouquet garni. Put in sweetbreads, cover and simmer gently on top of the stove for 25–35 minutes or bake in a moderate oven (350°F) for 35–45 minutes until sweetbreads are very tender.

To prepare garnish: blanch onions. Put them in a pan with 1 tablespoon butter and sugar and fry gently, shaking pan from time to time, until onions are tender and glazed with brown caramel. Skin the chestnuts (see box), add them

to the stock with remaining butter and simmer until cooked.

Watchpoint: barely cover chestnuts with stock and start to cook them with the lid on. After 20–30 minutes or when they are just tender, remove lid and continue cooking until stock is almost reduced and chestnuts are glazed; do not stir to avoid breaking them.

Fry croûtes and keep warm.

To serve: carve sweetbreads in diagonal slices and arrange them, overlapping, in a warm serving dish. Remove bouquet garni, bring sauce to a boil, taste for seasoning and spoon over sweetbreads. Garnish the dish with onions, chestnuts and fried croûtes.

For sweetbreads with chestnuts, brown the sweetbreads lightly in butter on all sides

---

To skin chestnuts: pierce each nut with a pointed knife. In a saucepan cover chestnuts with cold water, bring to a boil and take from heat. Lift nuts from water with a slotted spoon a few at a time; hold with a cloth and strip away shell and inner skin with a small sharp knife. If skin does not peel easily, put nut back in hot water for 1 minute longer.

Fritot of Sweetbreads

2–3 pairs (1½ lb) calves'
  sweetbreads
2 cups (½ lb) mushrooms
juice of ½ lemon
¼ cup seasoned flour (made
  with ¼ teaspoon salt, pinch
  of pepper)
deep fat (for frying)
sprigs of parsley (for garnish)
tartare sauce (for serving)

For fritter batter
¼ cup flour
pinch of salt
2 egg yolks
1 tablespoon melted butter or
  oil
½ cup milk
1 egg white

Method
Soak, blanch and trim the sweetbreads and press them between 2 plates until cold. Wipe mushrooms, trim stems level with the caps and sprinkle caps with lemon juice.

To make fritter batter: sift flour with salt into a bowl, make a well in the center and add the egg yolks and melted butter or oil. Add milk gradually, mixing to form a smooth batter, and beat thoroughly. Let stand in a cool place (not the refrigerator) for 30 minutes. Just before frying, whip the egg white until it holds a stiff peak and fold into the batter.

Slice or divide the sweetbreads into pieces and roll them in seasoned flour. Heat the deep fat until hot (375°F on a fat thermometer). Dip a few pieces of sweetbread into the batter, then fry them in the hot fat until browned. Drain them on paper towels and keep warm. Fry remaining sweetbreads and the mushroom caps in the same way, and pile them all in a warm serving dish. Let fat cool

slightly, then fry parsley for 10 seconds or until it stops sputtering; drain and scatter it on top of mushrooms and sweetbreads. Serve hot with the tartare sauce separately.

Tartare Sauce

2 hard-cooked eggs
1 uncooked egg yolk
salt and pepper
1½ cups oil
1–2 tablespoons vinegar
2 tablespoons chopped
  parsley
2 teaspoons chopped
  chives
2 teaspoons chopped
  capers or gherkin pickles

Method
Halve hard-cooked eggs, scoop out the yolks and work them through a sieve into a bowl. Add the uncooked egg yolk and seasoning and work together well. Add the oil drop by drop as for mayonnaise and when the mixture is very thick, stir in 1 tablespoon vinegar. Continue beating in the oil in a slow, steady stream until it is all added, stirring in more vinegar when the mixture becomes too stiff to work. Add herbs and capers or gherkin pickles, and season, adding more vinegar if necessary. If you like, add the shredded white of 1 hard-cooked egg.

Sweetbreads Soubise

2–3 pairs (1½ lb) calves'
    sweetbreads
3 tablespoons butter
1 onion, sliced
1 carrot, sliced
½ cup veal or chicken stock
½ cup white wine, or ½ cup
    more stock
1 clove of garlic, crushed
¼ teaspoon thyme
1 bay leaf
salt and pepper

For sauce
1 tablespoon butter
1 tablespoon flour
onion purée (made with 3 large
    Bermuda or mild onions,
    sliced, blanched and
    simmered in stock for 8–10
    minutes, then drained and
    puréed)
1–2 tablespoons heavy cream
    (optional)

To finish
1 cup (¼ lb) mushrooms, sliced
    and cooked in 1 tablespoon
    butter
½ cup (¼ lb) cooked ham, cut
    in strips
2 tablespoons grated Gruyère
    cheese

Method

Soak, blanch and trim sweetbreads and press them be-
tween 2 plates until cold.

In a skillet or shallow
flameproof casserole heat
butter and sauté sweetbreads
for about 5 minutes on each
side until lightly browned.
After turning them, add the
onion and carrot, shake pan
to prevent sticking and continue cooking until vegetables
are soft. Pour in stock, or
wine and stock, garlic, herbs
and seasoning, cover and
simmer on top of stove for
25–35 minutes or until sweetbreads are very tender. Remove and keep warm. Strain

and reserve liquid.

To make sauce: melt butter,
stir in flour and add liquid
from sweetbreads. Bring to a
boil, stirring, and add onion
purée; simmer 2–3 minutes
or until sauce coats the back
of a spoon. Add cream, if used,
and season to taste.

To finish: slice sweetbreads
diagonally in 2–3 pieces and
arrange in warm ovenproof
dish. Scatter mushrooms and
ham on top, spoon over sauce
and sprinkle with grated
cheese. Bake in a hot oven
(400°F) for 8–10 minutes or
until browned and serve
with boiled rice or mashed
potatoes.

Sweetbreads Bonne Maman

2–3 pairs (1½ lb) calves'
    sweetbreads
2 tablespoons butter
1½ tablespoons flour
2 cups veal or chicken stock
1 teaspoon tomato paste
salt and pepper
½ cup (¼ lb) chopped cooked
    ham
2 teaspoons chopped parsley
2–3 tablespoons heavy cream
mashed potatoes, made with
    3 boiled potatoes, ¼ cup
    butter, ½ cup scalded milk,
    salt and pepper (for piping
    border)
1 tablespoon grated Parmesan
    cheese (optional)

For julienne of vegetables
2 tablespoons butter
2 medium onions, chopped, or
    3 leeks, cut in julienne strips
3 carrots, cut in julienne strips
5–6 stalks of celery, cut in
    julienne strips
2 tomatoes, peeled, seeded
    and cut in strips

*Pastry bag with medium star
tube*

Method

Soak, blanch and trim sweetbreads and press them be-
tween 2 plates until cold.

In a shallow flameproof
casserole heat butter and
brown sweetbreads lightly
on all sides, remove them and
keep warm. Stir the flour into
the casserole, add stock,
tomato paste and seasoning
and bring to a boil, stirring.
Replace sweetbreads, cover
and bake in a moderate oven
(350°F) for 35–45 minutes or
until very tender.

To prepare julienne of
vegetables: melt butter in a
small shallow pan or flameproof casserole, add onion or
leek, carrot and celery, cover
with a piece of foil pressed
down on top, cover and cook
gently on top of the stove for
5 minutes. Then bake in
moderate oven (350°F) for
10–15 minutes longer until
vegetables are tender. Add
tomatoes with seasoning
and cook 2–3 minutes longer.

Remove sweetbreads, carve
in diagonal slices and arrange
them on the julienne of vegetables in a warm heatproof
serving dish. Keep warm.

Reduce sauce, if necessary,
until glossy and well-flavored,
skimming it well. Add chopped ham, parsley and cream,
reheat, taste for seasoning
and spoon over sweetbreads.

Fill mashed potato into the
pastry bag fitted with the star
tube and pipe a border of
mashed potato around the
dish.

Serve at once or, if you
like, sprinkle the dish with
grated Parmesan cheese and
brown for a few minutes in a
very hot oven (450°F).

Another recipe for sweet-
breads is given on page 76.

Sweetbreads Provençale

2–3 pairs (1½ lb) calves'
    sweetbreads
3 tablespoons butter
2 shallots, finely chopped
½ cup white wine
1½ cups well-flavored stock
salt and pepper
kneaded butter (made with
    1½ tablespoons butter,
    2 teaspoons flour)

For garnish
4 medium tomatoes, halved
    and seeded
6–8 green or ripe olives,
    pitted and chopped
½ cup (¼ lb) cooked ham,
    chopped
2 tablespoons chopped parsley
3 tablespoons mayonnaise

Method

Soak, blanch and trim sweetbreads and press them be-
tween 2 plates until cold.

In a skillet or shallow flameproof casserole melt butter
and brown sweetbreads on all
sides, add shallots and cook
until soft. Pour in the wine,
boil until reduced by half,
then add stock. Season, cover
and simmer gently on top of
the stove for 25–35 minutes
or bake in a moderate oven
(350°F) for 35–45 minutes.
Add the kneaded butter in
small pieces, shake to mix,
bring to a boil and cook 5
minutes longer or until sweetbreads are tender.

To prepare garnish: set tomatoes cut side up, in a buttered baking dish. Bake in a
moderate oven (350°F) for
5–10 minutes until thoroughly heated. Combine remaining ingredients, season and
pile in each tomato half. Broil
until browned, then keep hot.

Remove sweetbreads, carve
in diagonal slices and arrange
on a warm platter. Reduce
sauce, if necessary, until glos-

sy and well-flavored and spoon over sweetbreads. Garnish dish with tomatoes and serve.

Sweetbreads Dauphine

2–3 pairs (1½ lb) calves' sweetbreads
¼ lb piece of bacon
1 large onion, sliced
1 large carrot, sliced
½ cup white wine
salt and pepper
1½–2 cups well-flavored stock
1 tablespoon chopped parsley

For garnish
6–8 heads Belgian endive
2 tablespoons butter
6 tablespoons heavy cream

Method

Soak, blanch and trim sweetbreads and press them between 2 plates until cold. Chill them.

Cut the bacon in lardons (strips ¼ inch square and 1 inch long) and blanch. Make 3–4 incisions in each sweetbread with the point of a small knife and push in lardons.

Thoroughly butter a shallow casserole and put in onion and carrot with any remaining lardons. Arrange sweetbreads on top and pour around the wine. Season, cover and bake in a moderately hot oven (375°F) for 20–30 minutes. Then remove the lid, add 1½ cups stock and cook 15–20 minutes longer in a hot oven (400°F), basting frequently until the stock is very reduced so it almost forms a glaze and sweetbreads are tender. If the stock reduces before sweetbreads are tender, add a little more.

To prepare garnish: slice Belgian endive in ½ inch pieces. Spread a shallow pan with the butter, add endive pieces with seasoning, cover and cook gently 5–7 minutes until endive pieces are just tender; add the cream and keep warm.

Take out sweetbreads, cut in diagonal slices and arrange on a warm dish. Strain gravy, season to taste, and spoon over them, sprinkle with parsley and serve very hot, with endive served separately.

TONGUE

A whole tongue — fresh, corned or smoked — can be made into many delicious hot dishes or it can be pressed to serve for a cold buffet. Unlike most variety meats, the best tongue with a rich flavor comes from fullgrown beef cattle.

A beef tongue can weigh from 2–5 lb, but smaller tongues are considered the best. Calves' tongues tend to lack flavor, although they are tender — they are usually sold fresh and weigh from ½–2 lb. Lambs' tongues, weighing about ¼ lb, are sometimes available fresh or pickled; most pigs' tongues are used commercially. For 4 people, allow about 1½–2 lb uncooked tongue.

To cook a tongue: blanch it by putting in cold water, bringing to a boil and draining. Then return to the pan, cover with cold water, add 1 sliced onion, 1 sliced carrot, 2 stalks of celery, bouquet garni and 6 peppercorns, cover and simmer until very tender. Allow 3–4 hours for smoked or corned beef tongues, 2½–3½ hours for a fresh beef tongue, 1½–3 hours for fresh calves' tongues and 1 hour for fresh lambs' tongues.

To test if a tongue is cooked: pierce the thick part at the side with a skewer — if the skewer goes in easily, the tongue is ready. Also, if the root and its bones can be pulled out easily, this is another sign that the tongue is ready.

Transfer the tongue to a bowl of cold water and skin at once if tongue is to be served hot, or cool until tepid and then skin if tongue is to be served cold. The skin is hard to remove when the tongue is completely cold.

Reserve the strained stock from fresh tongues, to use in other dishes, but discard it from corned or smoked tongues as it is too salty to use. Slit the skin on the bottom side of the tongue and peel it off carefully. Pull out the small bones in the root and trim away the fat and gristle.

Watchpoint: it is essential that a tongue should be thoroughly cooked and tender — it is almost impossible to overcook.

The tongue is now ready for braising if it is to be served hot or it can be molded in a tongue press or springform pan to serve cold (see Volume 7). Cold beef tongue can also be sliced then reheated in a sauce such as sauce Madère or bigarade. Serve the dish at once if using smoked or corned tongue as the salt in it might spoil the flavor of the sauce. Cooked fresh tongue can be reheated and kept hot for a short time.

Pressed beef tongue should be carved in very thin slices to serve cold or in ¼ inch slices to be reheated. Carve unpressed beef tongue in diagonal slices across the tongue, starting at the tip and slanting the knife so the slices are of even size. Small calves' and lambs' tongues are carved from tip to root in 2–4 slices.

A tongue press has a round metal pan with a lid that can be screwed down to any level inside the pan. The tongue is curled inside pan while warm, the lid is screwed down as tightly as possible and tongue is chilled until firm, then unmolded in a neat round.

To line a large mold with aspic: set a clean, dry mold in a bowl of ice water. Pour about ½ cup cool but still liquid aspic into it and turn gently with a circular movement so aspic starts to coat the bottom and sides. When thick and just about to set, pour out any remaining aspic, turning mold so aspic can coat the sides. Repeat process until there is about a ¼ inch layer of aspic coating sides and base of mold. Add a little more cool aspic to the bottom and leave to set to form a ½ inch layer.

If adding a decoration, like sliced truffles or sliced hard-cooked egg white, dip them in cool aspic and place in base of mold and leave until set. Then carefully add another thin layer of aspic to set decoration firmly in place. Fill mold according to recipe (see calves' tongues Montmorency on next page).

Braised tongues bigarade (at back) are served with mashed potatoes, and calves' tongues Montmorency are garnished with cherry salad and watercress

Calves' Tongues Montmorency

2–3 calves' tongues (about 2 lb) or 1 small smoked or corned beef tongue
4 cups aspic, made with veal or chicken stock (see page 106)

For ham mousse
1 cup ($\frac{1}{2}$ lb) cooked lean ham
béchamel sauce, made with
    2 tablespoons butter,
    2 tablespoons flour, 1 cup milk (infused with slice of onion, 6 peppercorns, blade of mace and bay leaf) – chilled
1 envelope gelatin
$\frac{1}{4}$ cup aspic, made with veal or chicken stock
$\frac{1}{2}$ cup heavy cream, whipped until it holds a soft shape
salt and pepper

For cherry salad
1$\frac{1}{2}$ lb fresh Bing cherries, pitted or 1 can (1 lb) pitted cherries, drained
$\frac{1}{4}$ cup vinaigrette dressing (see page 61)
8–10 leaves of fresh tarragon or $\frac{1}{2}$ teaspoon dried tarragon
black pepper, freshly ground
bunch of watercress (for garnish)

Charlotte mold (1–1$\frac{1}{2}$ quart capacity)

Method
Blanch and simmer tongues until tender. Cool until tepid in cooking liquid, then skin and trim them. If large, cut tongues diagonally into $\frac{1}{4}$ inch slices; if small, slice them lengthwise. Line mold with aspic (see box on page 69). Arrange tongue slices on bottom and around sides of mold, line again with cool aspic and chill until set.

To make ham mousse: work ham twice through the fine blade of a grinder and

70

pound in a mortar and pestle with the chilled béchamel sauce until smooth. Or, instead of pounding, work ham with the béchamel sauce in a blender.

Sprinkle gelatin over $\frac{1}{4}$ cup cool but still liquid aspic, leave 5 minutes until spongy and dissolve over a pan of hot water. Stir into the ham mixture, then fold in whipped cream. Taste for seasoning and spoon the mousse into the lined mold. Cover and chill at least 3 hours or until set.

To prepare salad: toss the cherries with vinaigrette dressing. Add tarragon, a little black pepper and chill.

To serve: dip mold quickly in warm water and turn out on a platter. Surround with the remaining aspic, chopped, and garnish with the cherry salad and watercress or serve the salad separately.

For tongues Montmorency, spoon ham mousse into the mold, lined with aspic and cooked tongue slices

Braised Tongues Bigarade

2 lb fresh beef tongue or 2 calves' tongues (1 lb each)

For mirepoix
1 tablespoon butter
2 onions, diced
2 carrots, diced
1 medium turnip, diced
1 stalk of celery, diced
1$\frac{1}{2}$ cups well-flavored stock
bouquet garni

For Espagnole sauce (1$\frac{1}{2}$ cups)
3 tablespoons oil
2 tablespoons finely diced onion
2 tablespoons finely diced carrot
1 tablespoon finely diced celery
1$\frac{1}{2}$ tablespoons flour
$\frac{1}{2}$ teaspoon tomato paste
1 tablespoon chopped mushrooms
2$\frac{1}{2}$ cups well-flavored brown stock
bouquet garni
salt and pepper

For bigarade sauce
peeled rind and juice of 1 orange (preferably bitter Seville orange)
1 tablespoon butter
1 shallot, finely chopped
$\frac{3}{4}$ cup red wine
small bay leaf
1$\frac{1}{2}$ cups Espagnole sauce (as above)
2 teaspoons red currant jelly
squeeze of lemon juice (optional)

This whole dish can be prepared before and reheated just before serving. For the best flavor, this sauce should be made with a bitter Seville orange. If you use a sweet orange, sharpen the sauce with a few drops of lemon juice.

Method
Blanch and simmer tongue until tender; peel and trim it.

To make mirepoix: in a flameproof casserole heat butter and cook onion, carrot, turnip and celery, covered, over low heat for 5–7 minutes. Put prepared tongue on top, pour over stock, add bouquet garni, cover and bring to a boil. Braise in a low oven (300°F) for 1$\frac{1}{2}$–2 hours for beef tongue or 1 hour for calves' tongues or until very tender.

To make Espagnole sauce: in a saucepan heat oil and add diced vegetables. Lower heat and cook gently until vegetables are transparent and about to start browning; they will shrink slightly at this point. Stir in the flour and brown slowly, stirring constantly with a wire whisk or a metal spoon and scraping the flour well from the bottom of the pan. When it is a dark brown, cool slightly.
Watchpoint: do not allow flour to burn.

Stir in tomato paste, mushrooms, 2 cups cold stock, bouquet garni and seasoning. Bring to a boil, whisking constantly, partly cover pan and cook gently for 35–40 minutes. Skim off any scum. Add $\frac{1}{4}$ cup of remaining stock, bring to a boil and skim again. Simmer 5 minutes, add remaining $\frac{1}{4}$ cup stock, bring to a boil and skim again. (The addition of cold stock helps scum to rise to the surface and clears the sauce.) Cook 5 minutes longer, then strain, pressing vegetables gently to extract the juice.

To make bigarade sauce: in a small saucepan heat butter and cook shallot until soft. Add wine, bay leaf and rind of half the orange. Simmer gently until liquid is reduced by about one-quarter. Strain into Espagnole sauce, add red currant jelly and dissolve

over low heat.

Cut remaining orange rind into needle shreds and blanch in boiling water 5 minutes. Drain, refresh, drain and add with orange juice and lemon juice, if using, to sauce. Simmer 4–5 minutes and strain. Keep warm.

Take out the tongue and cut in $\frac{1}{4}$ inch slices. Strain cooking liquid, replace tongue in the braising pan and pour over the strained liquid. Return pan to a low oven (300°F) and continue cooking, uncovered, for 30 minutes, basting tongue with the liquid from time to time. By end of cooking it should look glazed.

Arrange tongue on a warm platter, spoon over a little bigarade sauce and serve the rest separately. Serve tongue with buttered green noodles or mashed potatoes.

For braised tongues bigarade, add the well-flavored stock to the tongues arranged on a vegetable mirepoix

Shoulder of lamb Normande (recipe is on page 76)

Start this week's party menu with a cream of onion soup, then roast a shoulder of lamb, stuffed with ground pork, apple and sage. Or you may prefer to serve sweetbreads with ham garnished with carrots in a cream sauce. The Russian tipsy cake, marbled with chocolate and decorated with rosettes of whipped cream, is a delicious ending to any menu.

Such richly-flavored alternatives for the main course require a full-bodied red wine. Few European wines will combine as well as a mature Côte Rôtie from France's Rhône Valley; these reds gain a special warmth and softness if they are between five and ten years old. America offers a suitable alternative in the Petit Syrah from California.

SERVE A STUFFED SHOULDER OF LAMB

Le Thourin
(Cream of Onion Soup)

Shoulder of Lamb Normande
Tomates au Fromage
Roast Potatoes
or
Sweetbreads Niquette
Potato Croquettes

Russian Tipsy Cake

Red Wine – Côte Rôtie (Rhône)
or Petit Syrah (California)

TIMETABLE

Day before
Make the tipsy cake. Cool and wrap in plastic bag.
Make chocolate caraque and store in airtight container.
Make breadcrumbs for lamb stuffing.
Make the soup but do not add liaison. Cover and refrigerate. Fry croûtons.
Or add the gelatin and sherry to the beef consommé and chill.

Morning
Bone and stuff the lamb and make the stock *or blanch and press sweetbreads.* Prepare tomatoes; peel and blanch potatoes for roasting *or peel carrots, boil potatoes for croquettes, mash them, and prepare croquettes, but do not fry.*
When sweetbreads are cold, simmer them for 20 minutes, drain and cool.

Assemble ingredients for final cooking from 6:15 for dinner around 8 p.m.

> You will find that **cooking times** given in the individual recipes for these dishes have sometimes been adapted in the timetable to help you when cooking and serving this menu as a party meal.

Order of Work
6:15
Set oven at moderately hot (375°F).
Make sugar syrup for cake.
6:30
Put lamb in oven to roast.
Split cake and soak layers with sugar syrup; fill and decorate with caraque and whipped cream.
6:45
Put potatoes in oven to roast: turn and baste lamb.
7:00
Baste lamb and turn potatoes.
Spoon consommé into cups, top with sour cream and caviar and chill.
7:30
Make béchamel sauce and keep warm; start to cook carrots; fry potato croquettes and keep hot.
7:45
Transfer lamb to platter and keep warm; put tomatoes in oven to bake.
Make gravy for lamb; keep warm.
Reheat soup and croûtons.
Drain carrots, add to béchamel sauce; pour on cream and keep warm.
Fry sweetbreads and keep warm; heat ham, reduce stock for sauce and arrange sweetbreads and ham on platter, with carrot garnish; keep warm.
Turn down oven and keep tomatoes warm.
Add liaison to soup.
8:00
Serve soup.
Garnish lamb with watercress, just before serving.

Le Thourin
(Cream of Onion Soup)

2 medium onions, thinly sliced
3 tablespoons butter
1½ tablespoons flour
4 cups milk
salt and pepper
2–3 slices of white bread, crusts removed, cut in cubes and fried in 3–4 tablespoons oil and butter, mixed (for croûtons)

For liaison
2 egg yolks
¼ cup heavy cream

Method
Melt the butter in a pan, add onion and stir to mix. Press a piece of foil on top, add a lid and sweat (cook very slowly) for 10–12 minutes or until onion is soft but not brown. Take pan from heat and stir in flour. Pour on the milk, add seasoning and bring to a boil, stirring. Cover pan and simmer 8–12 minutes.
Watchpoint: be sure to simmer the soup over very low heat; if it boils hard, the acid in the onion may curdle the milk.

Fry cubes of bread in hot oil and butter for a few minutes or until crisp and golden brown. Drain on paper towels, sprinkle lightly with salt, and reserve.

To prepare liaison: mix the egg yolks with the cream until smooth. Stir in about 2 tablespoons of the hot soup and stir this mixture into the remaining soup off the heat.

Reheat soup very carefully over a low heat until it thickens slightly — do not let it boil. Taste for seasoning, add a few croûtons to each bowl and serve the rest separately.

Consommé with Caviar

3 cans beef consommé
½ envelope gelatin
3 tablespoons sherry
black pepper, freshly ground

For serving
1 small jar red caviar
¼ cup sour cream
½ lemon, cut in 4 wedges

Method
Sprinkle the gelatin over ¼ can consommé and let stand 5 minutes until spongy. Dissolve gelatin over low heat and stir into the remaining consommé with sherry and black pepper to taste. Chill at least 3 hours or overnight. The consommé will be fairly firmly set.

A short time before serving, stir the consommé to break it up slightly and spoon it into chilled soup cups. Top each cup with 1 tablespoon sour cream and a spoonful of caviar. Place a wedge of lemon at the side and chill until ready to serve.

Serve le Thourin soup, made with milk and onions, with croûtons sprinkled on top

Entrée

Shoulder of Lamb Normande

small (4–5 lb) shoulder of lamb
¼ cup butter
½ cup white wine
1½ cups stock (made from
    lamb bones, root vegetables
    and seasoning)
1–2 teaspoons arrowroot
    (mixed to a paste with 1–2
    tablespoons water)
bunch of watercress (for
    garnish)

For stuffing
1 medium onion, chopped
2 tablespoons butter
1 cup fresh white breadcrumbs
½ lb ground pork
1 tablespoon chopped parsley
1 teaspoon sage
1 tart apple
salt and pepper
1 egg, beaten to mix

Method
Bone the shoulder of lamb
(or have the butcher do it for
you) and make stock with the
bones. Strain and reserve.

To make the stuffing: cook
onion in the butter until soft,
stir in breadcrumbs and let
cool. Add ground pork and
herbs. Pare the apple and
grate it on the coarsest side of
the grater. Stir into mixture
with plenty of seasoning and
add enough beaten egg to
bind the stuffing.

Set oven at moderately
hot (375°F).

Fill the stuffing into the
lamb, roll it up and tie in
several places with string.

Put the lamb in a roasting
pan, spread surface of the
meat with butter and pour in
the wine. Roast in heated
oven for 1½–1¾ hours or until
a meat thermometer inserted
in the center registers 160°F

*To bone shoulder of lamb,
use a small, sharp knife, cutting closely to the bone*

*After removing shoulder bone,
stuff lamb, roll up and tie with
string before roasting*

(for medium done meat).
Baste and turn the lamb from
time to time.

When the lamb is done,
transfer it to a hot serving
platter and keep warm. Discard all the fat from the roasting pan, leaving the meat
juices. Stir in about 1½ cups
of reserved stock and bring
to a boil, scraping the sides of
the pan well. Simmer about 5
minutes, strain and bring back
to a boil. Stir in just enough
arrowroot paste to thicken
slightly, taste for seasoning
and keep warm.

Remove string from the
lamb and moisten the meat
with a little gravy. Serve the
rest of the gravy separately.

Garnish the meat with
watercress and serve it with
roast potatoes and tomates
au fromage, topped with
cheese.

Accompaniment
to entrée

Tomates
au Fromage

4–6 medium tomatoes, peeled
salt and pepper
3 shallots, finely chopped
¾ cup grated cheese (preferably
    half Parmesan and half
    Gruyère)
2–3 tablespoons fresh white
    breadcrumbs
3 tablespoons melted butter

Method
Set the oven at moderately
hot (375°F).

Cut the tomatoes in half
crosswise and scoop out the
seeds. Season the halves and
place them, cut side up, on
an ovenproof dish. Sprinkle
the shallots on top. Mix the
cheese with the breadcrumbs
and cover each tomato half
with the mixture. Spoon

the melted butter carefully
over the top.

Bake tomatoes in heated
oven for about 10 minutes or
until they are tender but still
hold their shape.

Alternative
entrée

Sweetbreads
Niquette

2–3 pairs (about 1½ lb) calves'
    sweetbreads
2 slices of lemon
salt and pepper
¼ cup butter
1 onion, thinly sliced
1 carrot, thinly sliced
1½ cups well-flavored stock
8–10 thin slices of cooked ham

For garnish
1 lb baby carrots
thick béchamel sauce, made
    with 2 tablespoons butter,
    1½ tablespoons flour and
    ¾ cup milk (infused with slice
    of onion, 6 peppercorns,
    blade of mace and bay leaf)
2 tablespoons heavy cream

Method
Soak, blanch and press sweetbreads (see page 65).

Melt 2 tablespoons of the
butter in a shallow pan, add
onion and carrot, arrange
the sweetbreads on top, season and pour in the stock.
Cover and simmer 20 min-
utes. Remove sweetbreads
from pan; strain and reserve
stock; let sweetbreads cool.

To prepare garnish: leave
the baby carrots whole. Cook
them in boiling salted water
for 10–12 minutes or until
tender. Make the béchamel
sauce. Drain carrots and mix
with the béchamel sauce.
Pour the cream on top, cover

Sweetbreads Niquette are served with ham en couronne, and carrots in cream sauce

and keep in a warm place. The cream poured over the top prevents a skin from forming on the sauce.

Heat remaining 2 tablespoons butter in a skillet, add sweetbreads and fry carefully 2–3 minutes or until golden brown on both sides. Remove from pan; keep warm.

Put the ham slices in the same skillet and cook gently, 1–2 minutes, to heat them through. Cut the sweetbreads in diagonal slices. Arrange the ham en couronne (in a circle) with a slice of sweetbread on each slice of ham; keep warm. Pour the reserved stock into the skillet, bring to a boil and boil until reduced to about $\frac{1}{4}$ cup, then strain this gravy over the sweetbreads. Stir the cream into carrot garnish and spoon it into center of platter. Serve with potato croquettes.

Potato Croquettes

Cook 3 medium potatoes in boiling salted water for 15 minutes or until tender. Drain and work through a strainer or ricer. Return to pan and beat in 1 tablespoon butter, 1 egg yolk, 2 tablespoons hot milk, and salt and pepper. Cool mixture, and roll on a floured board into a 1-inch thick cylinder. Cut into 2-inch lengths. Roll croquettes in flour, seasoned with salt and pepper, and brush with 1 egg, beaten to mix with $\frac{1}{2}$ teaspoon salt. Coat with dry white breadcrumbs and fry in butter, turning so croquettes brown evenly, or fry in deep fat (375°F on a fat thermometer). Drain well on paper towels.

A dinner of le Thourin soup, shoulder of lamb Normande and a Russian tipsy cake (cut to show the marbling and filling), is served with a full-bodied red wine

Dessert

Russian Tipsy Cake

1 square (1 oz) unsweetened
   chocolate
3 tablespoons water
$\frac{1}{2}$ cup flour
pinch of salt
3 eggs
$\frac{1}{2}$ cup sugar
1 tablespoon more flour

For syrup
3 tablespoons sugar
$1\frac{1}{2}$ tablespoons water
3 tablespoons rum or brandy

For decoration
Chantilly cream (made with
   1 cup of heavy cream,
   stiffly whipped and flavored
   with 2–3 teaspoons sugar,
   $\frac{1}{2}$ teaspoon vanilla)
chocolate caraque (made with
   2 squares (2 oz) semisweet
   chocolate)

*9 inch springform pan; pastry
bag and medium star tube*

Method

Grease the pan, sprinkle with sugar, then with flour and discard excess. Set oven at moderately hot (375°F).

Melt unsweetened chocolate in the water over a low heat and stir until thick and creamy. Let stand until cool.

To make the cake: sift $\frac{1}{2}$ cup flour with salt. Beat eggs in a bowl until mixed and gradually beat in the sugar. Set the bowl over a pan of hot water and continue beating until the mixture is light and thick enough to leave a ribbon trail on itself when the beater is lifted. Take from the hot water and continue beating until cool. If using an electric beater, no heat is necessary. Fold in the flour with a large metal spoon and divide the batter in two.

Fold the melted chocolate into 1 portion. Add the extra tablespoon of flour to the other.

Put the 2 batters into the prepared pan, alternating spoonsful of the light and dark batter. Draw a knife through the batters to give a marbled effect. Bake in heated oven for 30–35 minutes or until the cake springs back when pressed lightly with a fingertip. Cool for a few minutes in the pan, then transfer the cake to a wire rack to cool completely.

To make syrup: heat sugar with the water until dissolved, cool it and add the rum or brandy.

Split the cake and spoon a little of the syrup over both layers. Sandwich the layers with the Chantilly cream, reserving some for decoration. Moisten the cake with remaining sugar syrup. Spoon remaining cream into the pastry bag fitted with the star tube and decorate the top with rosettes of cream and chocolate caraque.

Decorate tipsy cake with chocolate caraque and whipped cream after filling with cream

Lamb biriani is served with an onion and tomato salad (see page 89)

INDIAN AND PAKISTANI COOKING

Spices first came from India and Arabia. The cooking of India and Pakistan clearly reflects this heritage as almost all dishes are spiced. Curry is an example — it can be made with meat, poultry, vegetables or fish; it can be hot or mild, thick or thin with a bewildering choice of seasonings. The proportions are varied by the individual cook, so that a basic recipe may have literally thousands of interpretations.

Spices are used mainly to help preserve food in the hot, humid climate but they also add interest to a limited range of available ingredients. It is not surprising to find the most highly spiced dishes in the south, near the equator, and milder seasonings in northern India and Pakistan.

Indian and Pakistani cooking is greatly influenced by religious belief. Many Hindus are vegetarian, others do not eat fish; different castes are forbidden to eat together. Muslims have fewer dietary laws and are great meat eaters, though pork is forbidden.

In India, there is no single distinctive style of cooking. Each family cooks and eats according to the religious customs with which it was brought up — whether it is the vegetarian cooking of south India or the distinctive Moghlai cooking of north India; if the family moves, these customs go with it.

But the emphasis placed on preparing and serving food to visitors, no matter what the occasion, is maintained throughout India. Every important event — births, weddings — always includes a meal.

The conquerors of the sub-continent have left their mark on the cooking. The Persian love of nuts and sweet pastries is clearly shown in Indian desserts like jelabis — fritters garnished with pistachios and fresh rose petals. Many dishes have names derived from Persian — seekh kebabs, for instance (the word 'seekh' means 'nail or skewer' in Persian) and kofta kari — meatballs — comes from the Persian verb 'koftan', meaning to pound.

British influence is less successful — roast meat and two vegetables followed by steamed pudding is hardly a suitable diet for the sticky heat of India. British colonials were not used to heavily spiced food so they compromised by using local ingredients to make Indian-style dishes without the spices. Anglo-Indian curries may even be sweetened with apples.

The recipes that follow have been adapted for Western kitchens and tastes while trying to keep them as authentic as possible. Depending on the area from which they come, almost all the dishes would be more highly spiced when made in India.

Serving an Indian Meal

The traditional way to serve a meal is on a thali – a round metal tray. Some kind of bread is placed in the center with the other dishes in bowls around it. These may include spiced vegetables like eggplant, beans, cauliflower and potatoes, one or more kinds of curry, a bowl of dahi (curd) or a raita (vegetable with curd), several kinds of chutney, some dried hot chilies, a dish of dahl (lentil purée) and a large bowl of rice. Sometimes the rice is piled on the tray instead of bread.

In India and Pakistan food is eaten with the fingers of the right hand only. Because it is forbidden to touch anyone else's food, each person has an individual thali. After the meal, bowls of water are brought to the table to wash the hands.

Some kind of grain is served at all meals. Often this is rice, and a quarter of the cultivated land in India is devoted to its production. The more elaborate a menu, the more dishes and accompaniments are served; but rice is almost always included, sometimes plainly boiled, often cooked as a pilau. Other grains used are wheat and corn, particularly in the north where they are ground to make a variety of breads including chapatis, phulkas and parathas.

When considering Indian food, remember that the time spent in preparation is no object; in an Indian household there is always someone who can spend hours grinding spices for curries and grain for bread.

In India a meal ends with the making of 'paan' – a green betel leaf filled with crushed betel nut and herbs and spices such as cardamom and aniseed, folded and fastened with a clove. The paan is chewed as a digestive. Here, fresh fruit is probably the best ending to an Indian meal. You can serve it with an Indian-style dessert or candy, if you like.

Alcohol is not customary in India and Pakistan – the universal drink is strong black tea that turns bitter if it is infused for more than 15 minutes. Some coffee is grown in southern India, but the drink is almost unknown in the north. Soft drinks are very popular, some based on sweetened milk or buttermilk, others made with fruit like pineapple or lime, or vegetable juices like carrot or beets.

Indian and Pakistani Ingredients

Almost all the spices and ingredients needed for Indian and Pakistani dishes are available in good supermarkets. A few specialty items like tamarind can be found in Oriental and South Asian groceries.

Asafetida: dried resin from various plants, may be reddish-brown or beige. It has a powerful odor and a strong garlic-like flavor that is an acquired taste. (Asafetida may be omitted from any recipe.)

Cane sugar crystals (gur or jaggery): these crystals contain a little molasses. As a substitute, mix 1 cup dark brown sugar with 1 tablespoon dark molasses.

Cardamoms (illaichi): fruit of a reed-like plant. There are about 8 kinds; the best known are whitish pods that contain the black seeds used in cooking.

Chili pepper pod, dried (mirch): very hot small, dried red chilies. They are available whole and ground.

Chilies and peppers: soak fresh ones in cold salted water for 1 hour to remove some of the hot taste. Rinse canned chilies or peppers in cold water and drain them.

Coconut milk: comes from the flesh of fresh coconut. To make, steep freshly grated coconut in an equal quantity of boiling water for 30 minutes, then squeeze through cheesecloth to extract all the 'milk'.

Coriander (dhaniya): the aromatic green leaves of fresh coriander (sold in Latin American stores as cilantro) are chopped and added to salads and fresh chutney. Ground coriander seeds are used in curry.

Cumin (jeera): ground and whole cumin seeds are used to give an aromatic flavor reminiscent of caraway.

Curd (dahi): often used as a base for curry accompaniments. A close substitute is plain yogurt.

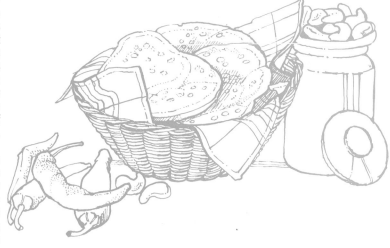

Curry powder: commercial curry powder is a blend of many spices including turmeric, coriander, cumin, fenugreek, black pepper and cayenne. Curry powder is not used in India, as there the spices are added individually in varying proportions, but it is convenient for seasoning mild curry soups and sauces.

Fenugreek (methi): slightly bitter seeds have odor of caramel.

Garam masala: Hindustani for mixed spice. It includes cinnamon, cloves, cardamoms, black cumin seeds, nutmeg and mace, usually ground together at home. It is obtainable in specialty stores.

Ginger root (adrak): chopped fresh or dried and ground, this is used in curries. Many Oriental stores carry fresh ginger root. To preserve, peel it, cut in pieces and pack in a jar with white vinegar to cover. This pickled ginger can be kept, tightly covered, for 1–2 months. — it is somewhat less fragrant than fresh ginger.

Legumes (dahl): a staple — many kinds both fresh and dried are used in Indian cooking. These include: pigeon peas or arhar dahl — resembling yellow split peas; chickpeas or chana dahl; masur dahl — similar to Egyptian lentils; mung beans or mung dahl; black-eyed peas or lombia dahl; red kidney beans or rajma dahl.

Mace (javatri): the lacy outer covering of the nutmeg. Its flavor is similar to but more aromatic than nutmeg; it comes in pieces (blades) or ground.

Poppy seeds (khaskas): sometimes used to thicken curries.

Rose water: a highly scented flavoring, made from fresh rose petals, that quickly loses strength if it is not tightly covered as the essential oils are very volatile. It is available at Middle Eastern and Oriental specialty stores.

Saffron (kesar): the most expensive spice which comes from stamens of autumn crocus — it gives a brilliant orange color to rice and curry dishes.

Tamarind (imli): the dried pulp from the pod of the tamarind tree, is added with a little crude sugar (gur) to give a sweet and sour flavor to curries. To use tamarind: infuse a piece the size of an egg in $\frac{1}{2}$ cup boiling water for 10 minutes, then squeeze it in a cheesecloth to extract the liquid. For a thicker infusion, use less water. To add extra tartness, use vinegar instead of water.

If tamarind is not available, substitute 1 tablespoon red currant jelly mixed with 1 tablespoon lemon or lime juice.

Turmeric (haldi): a pungent root that is ground and used to color and flavor curry. (Turmeric juice badly stains fabrics.)

Vinegar: use regular white, cider or white wine vinegars.

Ghee

Ghee is made from butter cooked for a long time over low heat to clarify it. In India ghee is used for frying whenever possible, but many families cannot afford it and use one of several vegetable oils instead. These are always used in vegetarian recipes. Vegetable oil can be substituted for ghee in all recipes.

Bombay Duck

This is a misleading name because it is not duck at all but a fish, salted and dried, available in cans.

It may be broiled until crisp or fried as an accompaniment to curry; the smell is pungent but the flavor is agreeably savory.

Huge baskets of the many kinds of spices are always on view at an Indian market — ground or ready for grinding in the home

In India rice is not the simple grain we think of – over 1,000 kinds are grown and different kinds are used for different dishes. India uses more rice than all the other countries of the world put together, except China.

Long grain rice is used in most recipes; Patna is the best and the regular grade among the families who can afford it.

Round grain rice is used for desserts. Other dishes may call for polished, pressed or puffed rice.

Rice flour is a common ingredient in breads and baking.

Fried Rice

1 cup rice, boiled
3 tablespoons ghee
1 medium onion, finely sliced
1 teaspoon ground turmeric
salt

Method
Melt the ghee in a skillet and fry the onion until golden brown. Add the turmeric and cook gently, stirring, for 1 minute. Stir in the rice with a fork, add a little salt and cook, tossing until the rice is well coated with oil. Cover tightly and bake in a moderate oven (350°F) for 8–10 minutes or until very hot.

Boiled Rice

1 cup long grain rice (preferably Busmati or Patna)
3 quarts water
juice of ½ lemon
1 tablespoon salt
3 inch stick of cinnamon
few whole cumin seeds (optional)
1 bay leaf

Method
In a large kettle bring the water to a boil with the lemon juice, salt, spices and bay leaf (tied in a cheesecloth bag). Sprinkle in the rice slowly so the water continues boiling. Boil without a lid for 10–12 minutes or until rice is tender. Drain at once into a colander, discard spices and bay leaf and rinse rice with plenty of boiling water to wash away the starch and separate the grains.

Stand the colander on a baking sheet in a very low oven (150°F–200°F) or in a warm place for 15 minutes. The grains should look snowy white and separate. If left longer, cover the colander with a cloth to prevent the top grains of rice from hardening.

A **pilau** or **pilaf** is a rice dish eaten in India, Persia and throughout the Middle East. The Indians call it pilau, but most western cooks are more familiar with the Turkish pronunciation – pilaf.

Saffron Rice

1 cup long grain rice, cooked for 8 minutes and drained (see boiled rice)
2 tablespoons ghee
¼ teaspoon mustard seed
½ cup blanched unsalted cashew nuts
½ tablespoon finely chopped fresh ginger root
large pinch of saffron, soaked in ¼ cup boiling water for 30 minutes
juice of 2 limes
1 tablespoon chopped fresh coriander
salt (optional)

Method
Heat the ghee and fry the mustard seeds until they burst. Add the cashew nuts and chopped ginger and cook until the nuts are brown. Mix fried nuts and seeds, rice, saffron liquid, lime juice and coriander. Stir well, transfer to a casserole, cover tightly and bake in a moderate oven (350°F) for 15 minutes or until the rice is tender and all the liquid is absorbed. Add salt to taste, if necessary.

The origin of 'curry' is the South Indian Tamil word 'kari' meaning sauce and, since an Indian sauce invariably contains spices, a curry has come to mean a spiced dish. The term covers a huge variety of fish, meat, poultry, egg and vegetable dishes. The basic ingredients often include ground turmeric to give color and flavor, chilies for hotness with ginger to temper the heat; garlic and onions for mellowness and tamarind or lime juice for acidity.

Spices such as coriander, cumin, cardamom and cloves, mustard and celery seed, cinnamon, saffron, nutmeg and mace, also aniseed, bay leaf, fennel and orange rind are common additions, depending on the recipe, and in the south, coconut milk is a regular ingredient.

The hotness of a curry varies with the region (the further north, the milder the curry) but heat is just one aspect of the flavor – equally important are mellowness and a balanced aftertaste in which no single flavor is predominant.

The procedure for a curry is simple – the spices are very finely ground (in India this is often done by hand each day, although ground spices will keep 3–6 months in an airtight container). The spices are added to the meat, vegetables or other main ingredients of the curry. Alternatively, the meat and vegetables may be fried in ghee (clarified butter) before the spices are added. Generally some kind of liquid is poured in, and the pan is tightly covered and cooked gently on top of the stove or in the oven.

Slow cooking is essential to develop the flavor of the spices and a shallow pan helps to evaporate and concentrate the cooking juices.

In India the timing of a curry is not of great importance — half an hour more or less does not make much difference to dishes that are cooked until ingredients are tender enough to cut with a spoon. The skill in cooking a curry lies in just the right balance of the spices and seasonings.

The following recipes have been adapted for Western tastes and cooking habits — the amount of chili has been reduced (some Indian curries use 20–30 chilies in a single dish) and exact measurements and cooking times are suggested. However, curry cooking is very much a matter of taste, so adjust and experiment as you go along.

Note: ghee is Indian clarified butter (see box on page 83). Many Indians cook with vegetable oil and this can be substituted for ghee in all recipes.

Garam Masala

two 3 inch pieces of cinnamon stick
$\frac{1}{4}$ cup whole cloves
1 cardamom pod
$\frac{1}{4}$ cup cumin seed
4 blades of mace
1 tablespoon coriander seed (optional)

The Western commercially-prepared curry powder follows the same principles as garam masala — a ground spice mixture for which each Indian cook has his own recipe.

Method
Set aside the cardamom pod. Spread the other spices in a roasting pan and bake them in a very low oven (200°F) for 25–30 minutes or until they are lightly toasted — do not let them become very brown. Cool them. Split the cardamom pod, scoop out the seeds and add to the baked spices.

Pound the spices in a mortar and pestle until they are very finely ground or work them, a little at a time, in a blender. Work the mixture through a sieve to remove any pieces and store in an airtight container. It will keep for 3–6 months.

Chicken Curry 1

3–3$\frac{1}{2}$ lb roasting chicken, cut in pieces
$\frac{1}{4}$ cup ghee
2 onions, sliced
seed of 1 cardamom pod
2 teaspoons ground coriander
$\frac{1}{2}$ teaspoon ground red chili pepper
1 teaspoon turmeric
1 teaspoon ground cumin
$\frac{1}{2}$ teaspoon ground ginger
1 tablespoon poppyseed, crushed
1$\frac{1}{2}$ cups chicken stock (made from giblets, neck and backbone of chicken)
salt
$\frac{1}{2}$ cup coconut milk
$\frac{1}{2}$ cup yogurt
squeeze of lime juice

Method
In a shallow flameproof casserole heat the ghee, add onion and cook until golden brown. Add the spices and poppyseed and cook gently 1 minute, stirring. Put the pieces of chicken flat in the pan, pour over stock, add a little salt, cover and simmer 30–40 minutes or until chicken is tender.

Remove the lid and reduce the liquid until it is fairly thick. Stir in the coconut milk and yogurt, bring to a boil, add the lime juice and more salt, if necessary, and simmer 2–3 minutes. Serve with rice and accompaniments of your choice.

Chicken Curry 2

3–3$\frac{1}{2}$ lb roasting chicken, cut in pieces
$\frac{1}{4}$ cup ghee
2 medium onions, finely chopped
1 clove of garlic, crushed
2 teaspoons finely chopped fresh ginger root
1 tablespoon ground coriander
1$\frac{1}{2}$ teaspoons ground cumin
$\frac{1}{2}$ teaspoon fenugreek seed, crushed
$\frac{1}{2}$ teaspoon turmeric
$\frac{1}{2}$ teaspoon ground red chili pepper
$\frac{1}{4}$ cup water
2 tomatoes, peeled, seeded and chopped
salt
1 teaspoon garam masala
1 tablespoon chopped fresh coriander
5 tablespoons infused tamarind or 1 tablespoon red currant jelly (mixed with juice of $\frac{1}{2}$ lemon and $\frac{1}{4}$ cup water)
6 whole blanched almonds, ground

Method
In a shallow flameproof casserole heat the ghee and brown the chicken pieces slowly on all sides. Remove them, add the onion, garlic and ginger and cook gently until the onion is golden brown. Add other spices with 1 tablespoon water; cook gently, stirring for 1 minute.

Stir in the tomatoes, remaining water and salt and replace the chicken. Sprinkle with garam masala and chopped coriander, cover and simmer 20–25 minutes or until the chicken is very tender. Mix the infused tamarind or the red currant jelly mixture with the ground almonds and stir into curry. To thicken sauce, boil mixture without covering. Taste for seasoning. Serve with rice and accompaniments of your choice.

Kofta Kari
(Curried Meatballs)

For meatballs
1½ lb ground lamb or beef
1 fresh or canned chili, cored, seeded and finely chopped
1 medium onion, finely chopped
1 clove of garlic, crushed
¼ cup plain yogurt
2 tablespoons chopped fresh coriander
2 teaspoons garam masala
¼ teaspoon ground mace or nutmeg
1 egg, beaten to mix
salt

For curry sauce
1 medium onion, finely sliced
2 tablespoons ghee
1 large tomato, peeled, seeded and chopped
1 teaspoon ground turmeric
1 teaspoon ground cumin
2 cloves of garlic, crushed
½ teaspoon ground red chili pepper (or to taste)
1 tablespoon chopped fresh ginger root
1 teaspoon salt
1 cup yogurt
¾ cup hot water
2 tablespoons chopped fresh coriander

This is one of the hotter curries.

Method
To make meatballs: mix all the ingredients except the egg. Add salt to taste. Work twice through the fine blade of the grinder and knead the mixture with the hand, adding enough beaten egg to bind it. Dampen your hands and roll the mixture into 1½ inch balls.

To make curry sauce: fry the onion in the ghee until golden brown. Add the tomato, turmeric, cumin and garlic and cook gently 2–3 minutes. Stir in the chili pepper, ginger and salt, then add the yogurt and simmer 15 minutes. Stir in hot water, taste for seasoning and carefully lower the meatballs into the sauce. Sprinkle the top with chopped coriander, cover, and simmer 30 minutes or until the meatballs are no longer pink in the center.

Egg and Lentil Curry

½ cup yellow Egyptian lentils or masur dahl (soaked overnight and drained)
1½ cups boiling water
½ teaspoon turmeric
½ teaspoon ground red chili pepper
1 onion, finely chopped
1 tablespoon oil
1 teaspoon ground coriander
1 teaspoon poppyseed, crushed
½ teaspoon ground cumin
1 cup coconut milk
salt
6 hard-cooked eggs
juice of 1 lime

Method
Put the lentils in a saucepan with the boiling water, turmeric and chili pepper, cover and simmer 1–1½ hours or until lentils are very soft. Beat with a whisk to a purée.

Fry the onion in the oil until golden brown, add the coriander, poppyseed and cumin and cook gently 2–3 minutes, stirring. Stir in the lentil purée with the coconut milk and a little salt and cook 1–2 minutes. Add the eggs, heat thoroughly, stir in the lime juice, taste for seasoning and serve with boiled rice and a raita or fresh chutney.

Shrimp Curry

1½ lb peeled, uncooked shrimps
1½ tablespoons ground coriander
1½ teaspoons ground cumin
½ teaspoon ground red chili pepper or to taste
¾ teaspoon ground turmeric
salt
1 clove of garlic, crushed
1–2 tablespoons water
2 tablespoons oil
2 medium onions, finely sliced
¼ cup coconut milk
1 cup fish stock or water
juice of ½ lemon
pinch of sugar

Method
Mix the spices, a little salt, and garlic to a paste with the water. In a skillet heat the oil and fry the onions until golden brown. Add the spice paste and cook 1–2 minutes, stirring — add 1 tablespoon water to prevent sticking if necessary. Add the coconut milk and fish stock or water and simmer gently 15–20 minutes or until the sauce is thick. Add the lemon juice and sugar, put in the shrimps and simmer 3–5 minutes until just cooked. Serve with rice and accompaniments of your choice.

Curried Brains

2 sets of lambs' brains
1 tablespoon vinegar
¼ cup ghee or oil
1 medium onion, sliced
½ teaspoon ground turmeric
½ teaspoon garam masala
½ cup coconut milk
½ cup water
salt
½ green pepper, cored, seeded and chopped
1 large tomato, peeled, seeded and chopped
1 tablespoon chopped fresh coriander
juice of ½ lime

Method
Soak brains in well-salted cold water for 2–3 hours, changing the water once or twice. Wash them thoroughly to remove all traces of blood, then blanch by putting them in cold water with the vinegar, bringing to a boil and draining. Rinse them and trim away any skin or membrane.

Put them in a saucepan in cold water, bring to a boil and simmer very gently for 15 minutes or until brains are firm to the touch; drain and cut each set in half.

Heat the ghee or oil and fry the onion until golden brown. Add the spices and cook, stirring, for 1 minute. Stir in the coconut milk and water with a little salt, add the brains, green pepper and tomato and sprinkle with fresh coriander. Simmer 10 minutes, sprinkle with lime juice, taste for seasoning and serve with chapatis and accompaniments of your choice.

Selection of Indian dishes includes (from left): boiled rice; spiced fish with stuffed tomatoes; banana and egg dish; poppadums and biriani. Accompaniments shown are: dahl; tomato salad; fried bananas and coconut; raita and mango chutney

Garam Machli
(Spiced Fish)

$1\frac{1}{2}$ lb cod, haddock or other
  firm white fish fillets
$\frac{1}{2}$ teaspoon ground red chili
  pepper
$\frac{1}{2}$ teaspoon ground turmeric
$\frac{1}{2}$ teaspoon salt
$\frac{1}{4}$ cup ghee

Method
Cut the fish into serving
pieces.

Mix the spices with the
salt and rub them into the
fish with the fingers. Cover
and let stand 30 minutes. In a
skillet heat the ghee and fry
the fish over medium heat for
2–3 minutes on each side
until it is brown and flakes
easily. Serve with accompaniments of your choice.

Tandoori Murgh
(Barbecued Chicken)

$3-3\frac{1}{2}$ lb roasting chicken
1 large onion, grated
3 cloves of garlic, crushed
1 tablespoon finely chopped
  fresh ginger root
1 teaspoon ground coriander
1 teaspoon ground cumin
pinch of ground red chili
  pepper (or to taste)
$1\frac{1}{2}$ teaspoons salt
$\frac{2}{3}$ cup plain yogurt
1 tablespoon vinegar
juice of 2 lemons
3 tablespoons melted ghee
1 teaspoon garam masala (see
  page 85)

A **tandoor** is a special oven
made from a huge heavy
earthenware pot. The pot is
filled with hot charcoal, then
buried until it has absorbed
the heat. The chicken is
inserted on a spit and cooked
by retained heat.

You can achieve similar
results by roasting the chicken
on a rotisserie.

Method
Slash the breast and legs of
the bird 3–4 times. In a mortar
and pestle pound the onion,
garlic and ginger to a paste
and work in the coriander,
cumin, ground chili pepper
and salt. Stir in the yogurt,
vinegar and the juice of 1
lemon. Alternatively, work
the onion, garlic, ginger, salt
and spices with the yogurt and
lemon juice in a blender. Rub
this mixture into the cuts in
the chicken, cover and leave
in the refrigerator for about
6 hours.

Brush the chicken with
melted ghee and roast it in a
moderately hot oven (375°F)
or on a rotisserie for $1\frac{1}{4}$–
$1\frac{1}{2}$ hours or until the bird is
tender and no pink juice runs
out when the thigh is pricked
with a fork; baste from time to
time with melted ghee. Alternatively, roast the bird in a
roasting pan, turning it from
time to time and brushing
with ghee.

To serve, carve the chicken,
brush it with the remaining
melted ghee and sprinkle over
the garam masala and the
remaining lemon juice.

Serve the chicken with
kachoomber (see page 93), or
with pilau rice and breads of
your choice. Garnish with
halved lemons, if you like.

*Tandoori murgh is delicious
barbecued chicken. Try it with
pilau rice and Indian breads
of your choice*

Korma
(Spiced Lamb)

$2\frac{1}{2}$–3 lb neck or riblets of lean
  lamb, cut in pieces
6 tablespoons ghee
4 medium onions, sliced
2 tablespoons ground coriander
$\frac{1}{2}$ teaspoon ground red chili
  pepper (or to taste)
1 cup water
salt
2 teaspoons garam masala (see
  page 85)
1 cup plain yogurt

Method
In a shallow flameproof casserole, melt the ghee and fry
the pieces of meat, a few at a
time, until browned on all
sides. Take out, add the onion
and fry until golden brown.
Remove half the onion and
reserve it. Add the coriander
and ground chili pepper to the
pan and cook gently, stirring,
for 1–2 minutes. Replace the
meat, add water and a
pinch of salt, cover and simmer 1 hour or until meat is
almost tender.

Mix the garam masala with
yogurt and pour over the meat
with reserved onion. Stir
until mixed, then simmer
uncovered 15–18 minutes
or until liquid is thick. Adjust
seasoning and serve with
rice and accompaniments
of your choice.

Biriani, a mixture of lamb curry and rice, is garnished with almonds and raisins

Lamb Biriani
(Lamb with Rice)

1½–2 lb boned leg of lamb, cut
   in 2 inch cubes
1½ cups long grain rice
   (preferably Busmati or
   Patna)
4 fresh or canned green
   chilies, cored, seeded and
   finely chopped
1 clove of garlic, crushed
2–3 stems of fresh coriander or
   sprigs of mint
2 teaspoons ground cumin
¼ teaspoon cayenne
1 teaspoon garam masala
   (see page 85)
½ cup plain yogurt
⅓ cup ghee
4 medium onions, thinly sliced
2 cups water
1 teaspoon salt
pinch of saffron
1 cup hot milk
3 medium potatoes, boiled and
   quartered
½ cup slivered almonds
½ cup raisins

Biriani is a combination of
rice with a fish, chicken or
meat curry.

Method

Mix the chilies with the garlic,
coriander or mint, and other
spices and stir in the yogurt.
Add the cubed lamb, mix well,
cover and let marinate for
1–2 hours.

In a shallow flameproof
casserole heat ¼ cup ghee and
fry the onions until golden
brown. Take onion from the
pan and brown the meat, a
few pieces at a time, on all
sides. Put all the meat in the
pan, add the water and salt,
cover and simmer 1–1½ hours
or until the lamb is very tender.
until the lamb is very tender.

To cook the rice: let the
saffron infuse in the hot milk
for 10 minutes. Boil the rice
in plenty of boiling salted
water for 10 minutes only,

drain and dry as for boiled rice
(see page 84).

When the meat is tender,
reduce the sauce, if necessary, until fairly thick, then
add half the fried onion and
one-quarter of the rice.
Moisten with 2–3 table-
spoons of the saffron-flavored
milk and layer the mixture
alternately with the potatoes
and rice finishing with a layer
of rice. Sprinkle the remaining
saffron milk on top. Cover
with dampened cheesecloth
to keep the rice moist, add
the lid and bake in a moderate
oven (350°F) for 30 minutes.

Fry the almonds in the remaining ghee until beginning
to brown, add the raisins and
cook 1 minute longer or until
the almonds are browned and
the raisins plump.

To serve the biriani, scatter
over the remaining onion and
sprinkle the raisins and
almonds on top. Serve with
kachoomber (see page 93).

Sabzi Ka Chaval
(Rice and Fresh
Vegetable Pilau)

1½ cups long grain rice
5 tablespoons ghee
1 large onion, finely chopped
1 teaspoon ground turmeric
4 cups water
1 medium potato, cut in ½ inch
   cubes
1 medium green bell pepper,
   cored, seeded and cut in
   thin strips
1 medium cauliflower, divided
   into sprigs
1 cup shelled fresh green peas
3 tomatoes, peeled, seeded and
   chopped
1 teaspoon garam masala (see
   page 85)
salt
1½ tablespoons finely chopped
   fresh coriander

Method

In a flameproof casserole heat
half the ghee and fry the
onions over medium heat
until golden brown. Stir in
the turmeric and continue
cooking 1 minute. Add the

rice and stir until the grains
are coated with ghee and turmeric. Pour in the water, add
the vegetables and tomatoes,
the garam masala, and a little
salt, cover the pan and bring
to a boil. Simmer 20 minutes
or until the vegetables and rice
are tender and all the liquid
has been absorbed. Taste for
seasoning.

To serve: pile the rice mixture on a hot serving dish
and sprinkle the top with the
remaining ghee and the chopped coriander.

KEBABS

Kebabs are a favorite Muslim dish, and innumerable kinds of kebab are served in northern India and Pakistan.

Seekh Kebabs

1½ lb boneless leg of lamb, cut in 1 inch cubes
1 medium onion, very finely chopped
1 clove of garlic, crushed
½ teaspoon poppyseed, crushed
1 teaspoon garam masala (see page 85)
½ teaspoon ground red chili pepper
½ teaspoon ground turmeric
salt
½ cup yogurt
1 tablespoon lemon juice
¼ cup melted ghee

8–10 kebab skewers

Method
Mix the onion with the garlic, poppyseed, spices and a little salt. Stir in the yogurt and lemon juice, add the meat and stir to mix well. Cover and let marinate 6–8 hours, then thread the meat on skewers so the pieces do not quite touch each other and brush with ghee. Broil 5–6 inches from the heat for 10–12 minutes or until no trace of pink shows when the meat is pierced, turning the kebab skewers from time to time. Serve with pilau and accompaniments of your choice.

Shami Kebabs
(Curried Meatballs)

1¼–1½ lb ground lamb or beef
1 medium onion, very finely chopped
1–2 fresh or canned green chilies, cored, seeded and very finely chopped
1 clove of garlic, crushed
1 medium potato, boiled and mashed
1 teaspoon garam masala (see page 85)
2 teaspoons thick infused tamarind
1 tablespoon finely chopped fresh ginger root
salt
¼ cup ghee
2 large onions, thinly sliced in rings (for garnish)

8–10 kebab skewers (optional)

Method
Combine all the ingredients, except the ghee and the onion rings. Add salt to taste and knead with the hand to a smooth mixture. Shape into balls the size of a walnut and flatten them slightly. Heat the ghee and fry the balls over medium heat for 10–12 minutes or until they are no longer pink in the center, turning them so they brown evenly.

Alternatively, the meatballs may be threaded carefully on skewers, brushed with ghee and broiled 5–6 inches from the heat, basting with more ghee and turning occasionally for 8–10 minutes or until no longer pink in the center. Scatter sliced onion rings over the kebabs and serve with rice and accompaniments of your choice.

Parsee Khichri with Shrimps

¾ lb uncooked peeled shrimps
⅓ cup Egyptian lentils or masur dahl (soaked overnight and drained)
3 tablespoons ghee
4 medium onions, sliced
5 fresh or canned green chilies, cored, seeded and chopped
4 fresh red chilies, cored, seeded and chopped
4 cloves of garlic, crushed
1 tablespoon chopped fresh ginger root
1 teaspoon ground cumin
½ teaspoon ground turmeric
3 tomatoes, peeled, seeded and chopped
2 cups water
¾ cup long grain rice
salt

Method
In a shallow flameproof casserole heat the ghee and fry the onions until golden brown. Add the chilies, garlic, ginger, cumin, turmeric and tomatoes and cook gently 2–3 minutes. Stir in the shrimps and continue cooking 2–3 minutes until the shrimps are pink. Add the water, then stir in the rice and soaked lentils. Cover the pan and simmer gently for 25–30 minutes until all the water is absorbed and the lentils and rice are tender. Season to taste.

> **The Parsees** (or Zoroastrians) settled around Bombay over 1,000 years ago when they fled from persecution in Persia. They have kept their religious practices, but combined their customs with Indian ones and are now the most westernized of Indians. Their leader is the Aga Khan.

Parsee Eggs

4 eggs
2 egg yolks
3 tablespoons ghee
1 medium onion, finely chopped
2 teaspoons finely chopped fresh ginger root
2 tablespoons chopped fresh coriander
1 fresh or canned green chili, cored, seeded and finely chopped
1 clove of garlic, crushed
salt
2 tablespoons infused tamarind

For garnish (optional)
1 tomato, peeled and cut in wedges
1 tablespoon chopped fresh coriander

Method
In a skillet heat the ghee and fry the onion and ginger until golden brown. Beat the eggs and yolks until thoroughly mixed with the coriander, chili and garlic. Add a large pinch of salt and the infused tamarind and pour into the pan. Cook over very gentle heat, stirring, until the eggs are creamy and just set. Continue cooking 20–30 seconds, then slide the 'omelet' onto a hot platter.

Garnish the top with wedges of tomato and chopped fresh coriander, if you like, and serve with parathas (see page 97).

Note: ghee is Indian clarified butter (see box on page 83). Many Indians cook with vegetable oil and this can be substituted for ghee in all recipes.

Parsee eggs are spiced with coriander, green chili, garlic and ginger

Anglo-Indian Banana and Egg

6 bananas
6 eggs
2 medium onions, finely sliced
3 tablespoons ghee
2 tomatoes, peeled, seeded and chopped
1 fresh or canned green chili, cored, seeded and finely chopped
1 tablespoon chopped fresh coriander
$\frac{1}{2}$ teaspoon ground turmeric
1 clove of garlic, crushed
$\frac{1}{2}$ teaspoon salt

When India was part of the British Empire, a new kind of cooking evolved – the cooking of the Raj or Anglo-Indian cooking – when European dishes were prepared by Indian cooks.

Method
Fry the onion in the ghee until golden brown. Peel and slice the bananas about $\frac{1}{2}$ inch thick and add to the pan with the remaining ingredients except the eggs; cook gently until the bananas are soft.

Spread the mixture in a shallow baking dish, make 6 hollows, break the eggs into them and dot the tops with the remaining ghee. Bake in a moderate oven (350°F) for 10–15 minutes or until the eggs are just set.

For Anglo-Indian banana and egg, break eggs into hollows in banana mixture before baking

SAMBALS

(Accompaniments)

The sambals or accompaniments at an Indian meal are just as important as the main dish – in fact, it is often difficult to pick out any one dish as the most important. The more elaborate the menu, the more accompaniments are served. They are carefully chosen to complement each other and include hot and cooling flavors, smooth and crisp textures and an appealing contrast of colors.

Some accompaniments can be grouped in special categories; for instance, chutneys and pickles, dried pea and bean dishes, and raitas or dishes made with curd. However, there are many other fruit and vegetable accompaniments.

Banana and Coconut Sambal

3 bananas
2 tablespoons grated fresh coconut
1 tablespoon lemon juice
pinch of salt
pinch of sugar

Method
Peel bananas and cut in $\frac{1}{4}$ inch slices. Sprinkle with lemon juice, salt and sugar and top with grated coconut.

Dahl
(Legumes)

Both fresh and dried peas and beans are used throughout India and Pakistan and scarcely any meal is served without a sambal or main dish containing some kind of legume. These are particularly important as they provide the principal source of protein for the huge vegetarian population of southern India.

Dahl purée, made from any of a number of dried peas or beans, including chick-peas and kidney beans, is served at most Indian meals as a bland accompaniment to balance the fiery heat of curry.

Chana Dahl
(Chick-pea Purée)

1 cup chick-peas (soaked overnight and drained)
$\frac{1}{4}$ cup ghee
1 medium onion, finely sliced
1 teaspoon ground cumin
$\frac{1}{2}$ teaspoon ground ginger
$\frac{1}{2}$ teaspoon ground red chili pepper
1 teaspoon garam masala (see page 85)
1 small potato, boiled and diced
1 tablespoon thick infused tamarind
salt
pinch of sugar

Method
Simmer the chick-peas in water to cover in a covered pan for 1–1$\frac{1}{2}$ hours or until soft. Drain them, reserving the liquid. In a skillet heat the ghee and fry the onion until golden brown. Add the spices, except tamarind, and cook gently, stirring, for 1–2 minutes. Stir in 1 cup of the reserved liquid, add the chick-peas and diced potato and bring just to a boil. Add infused tamarind, with salt and sugar to taste, simmer 10 minutes and serve.

A **sambar** is a legume purée cooked with vegetables and spices, a vegetarian dish that may also form part of a meat meal.

Masur Dahl
(Lentil Purée)

1 cup Egyptian lentils or
   masur dahl (soaked
   overnight and drained)
2½–3 cups stock
½ teaspoon ground red chili
   pepper
½ teaspoon turmeric
pinch of ground asafetida
   (optional)
salt
2 tablespoons ghee
1 small onion, finely chopped
½ teaspoon chopped fresh
   ginger root
1 teaspoon garam masala
   (see page 85)

For garnish
2 tablespoons ghee
2 onions, finely sliced

Method
Put the lentils in a saucepan
with 2½ cups stock, chili
pepper, turmeric and asafetida, if used; cover, bring to a
boil and simmer 1–1½ hours
or until the lentils are very
soft. Beat with a whisk or
wooden spoon until the
mixture is a purée, adding a
little salt, and more stock if
necessary – the consistency
should be soft and smooth,
not sticky or soupy.
  In a skillet heat the ghee,
add the onion and cook until
golden brown. Stir in the
ginger and garam masala and
cook, stirring, for 2–3 minutes. Add to purée and taste
for seasoning.
  In a skillet melt the 2 tablespoons ghee and fry the onion
slices until golden brown;
drain and sprinkle on top of
purée.

Arhar Sambar
(Split Peas
with Vegetables)

1 cup yellow split peas or
   arhar dahl (pigeon peas)
   – soaked overnight and
   drained
1 onion, thinly sliced
2 fresh or canned green
   chilies, cored, seeded and
   chopped
5 cups water
2 tablespoons oil
1 tablespoon mustard seed
1 tablespoon ground coriander
½ teaspoon ground red chili
   pepper
½ teaspoon ground cumin
½ teaspoon ground turmeric
salt
pinch of asafetida (optional)
1 green bell pepper, cored,
   seeded and sliced
2 tomatoes, peeled, seeded
   and coarsely chopped
10–12 small onions, peeled
1 cup green beans, cut in
   1 inch pieces
½ cup grated fresh coconut
⅓ cup infused tamarind

Method
Put the peas in a pan with the
thinly sliced onion, chilies and
water, cover and bring to a
boil. Simmer 1 hour. In a small
pan heat the oil, add the
mustard seeds and cook until
they burst; add the coriander,
chili pepper, cumin, turmeric,
a little salt, and asafetida if
using, and continue cooking
gently for 2 minutes. Stir this
mixture into the peas with the
green pepper, tomatoes, small
onions and green beans.
Cover and continue cooking
25–30 minutes or until the
peas are very soft but not
mushy. Stir in the coconut
and infused tamarind, simmer
2–3 minutes, add more salt,
if necessary, and serve.

Tomato Bhartha

4 ripe tomatoes, peeled,
   seeded and coarsely
   chopped
2 fresh or canned green chilies,
   cored, seeded and chopped
1 medium onion, very finely
   chopped
salt
sugar
juice of ½ lemon
1 tablespoon chopped
   fresh coriander

A bhartha is a Muslim savory
dish served with rice.

Method
Combine tomatoes, chilies
and onion. Season to taste
with salt, sugar and lemon
juice and sprinkle with
chopped coriander.

Simla Belati
(Stuffed tomatoes)

4 tomatoes
2 tablespoons ghee
2 onions, sliced
1 fresh or canned green chili,
   cored, seeded and chopped
1 teaspoon ground cumin
salt
½ cup browned cashew nuts

Method
In a skillet or pan heat the
ghee and fry the onion until
golden brown. Add the chili,
cumin and a little salt and
cook gently for 2 minutes.
Cut the tops from the tomatoes, scoop out the seeds and
work through a sieve to
extract the juice; add juice to
the chili mixture and simmer
2 more minutes. Stir in the
nuts and put the mixture
into the tomatoes.
  Replace the tomato tops
and bake in moderate oven
(350°F) for 10–15 minutes
or until tomatoes are just
cooked.

Kachoomber

2 onions, chopped
2 tomatoes, peeled, seeded and
   chopped
1 cucumber, peeled, seeds
   removed and diced
1 fresh or canned green chili,
   cored, seeded and chopped
2 tablespoons vinegar (or to
   taste)
salt and sugar (to taste)
1 tablespoon chopped fresh
   coriander

Many vegetables and fruits
can be used to make a
kachoomber – a raw salad
flavored with fresh herbs.

Method
Mix the onion, tomato,
cucumber and chili with the
vinegar. Season with salt and
sugar; sprinkle with chopped
coriander.

To Prepare Peppers
and Chilies
Dried chilies: wash in cold
water, remove veins, stems
and seeds and cut chilies into
small pieces. Pour on about
6 cups boiling water per cup
of chilies and add 2 teaspoons
vinegar. Let soak for about 30
minutes and drain, reserving
liquid if necessary.
Fresh chilies: soak in cold
salted water for 1 hour to
remove some of the hot taste
and drain. Use rubber gloves
when handling fresh chilies as
they contain oils that irritate
the skin.
Canned chilies: rinse in cold
water and drain, reserving
liquid, if necessary.

Tomato bhartha is a mixture of tomatoes, chilies and onions (recipe is on page 93)

Raitas

Raitas are the most cooling accompaniments to curry. They are based on dahi (curd), made of sour milk — yogurt is a close substitute.

Cucumber Raita

2 cucumbers
salt
1 fresh or canned green or red chili, cored, seeded and chopped
½ onion, finely chopped
1 cup plain yogurt
1 tablespoon fresh chopped coriander

Method
Peel the cucumbers and shred on a coarse grater; sprinkle lightly with salt, cover and let stand 1 hour. Press with a plate to draw out juices (dégorger). Mix in the chili, onion, yogurt and coriander and season with more salt, if necessary.

Eggplant Raita

1 medium eggplant
2 tablespoons ghee
1 medium onion, finely chopped
2 tomatoes, peeled, seeded and chopped
1 tablespoon finely chopped fresh ginger root
1 teaspoon ground coriander
1 cup plain yogurt
salt

Method
Rub the eggplant skin with a little ghee and bake it in a moderate oven (350°F) for 45 minutes or until very soft. Cool it, then peel it and coarsely chop the pulp. In a skillet heat the remaining ghee and fry the onion until golden brown. Stir them into the eggplant pulp with the tomatoes, ginger root, coriander, yogurt and salt to taste.

Mattar Paneer
(Indian Cheese with Peas)

1½ cups shelled fresh green peas, or 1 package frozen peas, thawed
1 cup paneer (see box)
6 tablespoons ghee
1 teaspoon turmeric
1 teaspoon ground red chili pepper
2 tablespoons chopped fresh coriander
salt
sugar (optional)

This is a vegetarian dish that may also form part of a meat meal.

Method
Make the paneer. In a skillet or pan heat the ghee, add the peas with the turmeric and chili pepper and cook, stirring, for 3 minutes over medium heat. Add the paneer, which should look like dry cottage cheese, mix well and cook gently 2 minutes. Stir in the chopped coriander with salt to taste and cook just below simmering point for 10 minutes or until the peas are tender. If the cheese is very acid, add a little sugar.

Note: ghee is Indian clarified butter (see box on page 83). Many Indians cook with vegetable oil and this can be substituted for ghee in all recipes.

To Make Paneer (Indian Cheese)

For 1 cup: scald 2 quarts milk, take from heat and stir in 2 teaspoons powdered alum (obtainable from pharmacies). Return to heat and stir, without boiling, for 10–12 minutes or until milk curdles and separates completely.

Transfer to a colander lined with cheesecloth and drain off most of the whey. Then lift the cheesecloth, twisting the ends to squeeze all the remaining whey from the cheese — it should be crumbly and as dry as possible.

Spiced Potatoes

3–4 medium potatoes
1½ tablespoons oil
1 teaspoon mustard seeds
½ teaspoon turmeric
1 teaspoon cumin seeds
1 fresh or canned green chili, cored, seeded and chopped
1 tablespoon chopped fresh coriander
juice of 1 lime

Method
Cook the potatoes in their skins in boiling salted water for 15–20 minutes or until just tender. Peel them and cut in chunks while still hot. In a skillet heat the oil and add the potatoes with the mustard seeds, turmeric, cumin and chili. Cook gently, turning the potatoes carefully, for 2–3 minutes or until they are very hot and all the oil is absorbed. Take from the heat, sprinkle with fresh coriander and lime juice and serve.

PICKLES AND CHUTNEYS

Pickles and chutneys are typically Indian and the word chutney comes from the Hindu 'chatni'. All good Indian cooks make their own chutneys and serve several – hot or mild, fresh or pickled – at every main meal.

Recipes for **tomato chutney**, **piccalilli** and **mustard pickle** are given in Volume 11 and these can be served with Indian-style meals.

Fresh Mango Chutney

1 ripe mango
1 fresh or canned green chili, cored, seeded and finely chopped
1 teaspoon finely chopped fresh ginger root
1 tablespoon grated onion
1 tablespoon vinegar
pinch of salt
pinch of sugar

This chutney should be used within a day of making.

Method

Peel the mango over a bowl, cut the flesh from the pit and crush with a fork. Add the chili, ginger and onion, sprinkle over the vinegar, salt and sugar, stir well and taste for seasoning.

Cooked Mango Chutney

6 barely ripe mangoes
1 cup raisins
$\frac{1}{4}$ cup chopped fresh ginger root
pinch of ground red chili pepper
$\frac{1}{2}$ teaspoon cumin seed
1 tablespoon salt
2 cloves of garlic, crushed
3 tablespoons lemon or lime juice
2 cups white vinegar
2 cups sugar

This cooked mango chutney can be sealed and stored for up to 6 months.

Method

Peel the mangoes over a bowl and cut the flesh from the pits in slices. Put the slices and juice in a stainless steel pan or preserving kettle with the raisins, ginger, spices, salt, garlic and lemon or lime juice. Pour over the vinegar, add the sugar and heat gently until the sugar dissolves. Bring to a boil and simmer until chutney is thick and mango slices look transparent. Pour chutney into hot dry jars, and seal at once.

Fresh Coconut Chutney

1 cup grated fresh coconut
1 tablespoon chopped fresh ginger root
2 fresh or canned green chilies, finely chopped
2 tablespoons chopped fresh coriander
2 teaspoons mustard seed (optional)
3–4 tablespoons lemon juice

This chutney is ready to use and can be kept for up to a week in the refrigerator.

Method

Pound the coconut and ginger in a mortar and pestle or work them in a blender until smooth. Mix in the chilies, coriander and mustard seed with enough lemon juice to make a paste.

Sharp Lemon or Lime Pickle

7 juicy lemons with their skins, or 10 limes
juice of 4 limes
$1\frac{1}{2}$ tablespoons salt
1 teaspoon crushed mustard seed
2 teaspoons crushed red pepper
3 tablespoons chopped fresh ginger root
2 teaspoons crushed bay leaf

This pickle is ready to use after a week but can be kept in a cool place for up to 6 weeks.

Method

Wash and dry the lemons or limes; roll them firmly on the table with your hand to soften them slightly, then cut in quarters, discarding the hard ends and seeds. In a jar arrange a layer of limes or lemons, sprinkle with salt, mustard seed, red pepper, ginger and bay leaf. Continue making layers until all the ingredients are used, then pour over the lime juice, cover the jar, shake well and leave, covered with a cloth, at room·temperature.

Parsee Shrimp Pickle

2 lb uncooked, peeled shrimps
2 teaspoons salt
3 tablespoons finely chopped fresh ginger root
3 tablespoons crushed garlic cloves
1 tablespoon ground cumin
4–6 fresh red chilies, cored, seeded and finely chopped
2 cups vinegar
1 cup oil
2 tablespoons dry mustard
2 tablespoons ground allspice
1 tablespoon gur (cane sugar crystals) or to taste
1 teaspoon ground turmeric

Keeps for 6–8 weeks.

Method

Sprinkle the shrimps with salt, cover and let stand 30 minutes. In a mortar and pestle pound the ginger, garlic, cumin, and chilies together and stir in 1 cup vinegar – or purée the ginger, garlic, cumin and chilies together with the vinegar in a blender.

Press the shrimps between 2 plates to remove all the liquid. Put them in a saucepan and toss quickly over medium heat until dry. Add the vinegar mixture and simmer 4–5 minutes. Stir in the oil, bring just to a boil, take from the heat and let cool.

Stir in the mustard, allspice, gur to taste, remaining vinegar and turmeric, mix well and pack into jars.

BREADS

Most Indian breads are un-leavened, flat and circular. Wheat is the most common flour, though rye, rice, corn and barley may also be used. Some breads are baked in the oven, others are cooked on a griddle or fried and they may be soft like chapatis and parathas or crisp and brittle like puris and poppadums.

The same basic dough can be used for chapatis, phulkas, parathas or puris though recipes vary from region to region. They should be cooked just before serving and many of them must be hot to be at their best.

Chapatis

2 cups wholewheat flour
1 teaspoon salt
3 tablespoons ghee or butter
10—12 tablespoons lukewarm
water

Tawa or griddle

A **tawa** is used in India for making chapatis; it is a slightly concave iron disc, 8—9 inches in diameter and only about one-twelfth inch thick, that is placed over the open fire. Butter can be substituted for ghee in this recipe. Makes 9—10 chapatis.

Method
Mix the flour and salt on a board, add the ghee or butter and rub in with the fingertips until the mixture resembles crumbs. Add 8 tablespoons water and mix to a pliable dough, adding more water as necessary. Knead the dough thoroughly for 8—10 minutes, cover with a damp cloth and

let stand 2 hours.

Divide the dough into 9—10 pieces and roll them into balls. On a floured board, roll out the balls to very thin circles about 8—9 inches in diameter and cover each one with a cloth as it is rolled.

Gently heat the tawa or griddle. Place a chapati on it, press down lightly and continue cooking for 2—3 minutes or until it has brown spots underneath. Turn it over and brown on the other side.

Just before serving, broil the chapatis, placing them 6—7 inches from the heat for $\frac{1}{2}$ minute or until they puff up in patches. (In India they are placed on the coals.)

Chapatis may be kept hot for a few minutes after cooking by covering with a cloth but they should be eaten as soon as possible.

Poppadums

Poppadums are thin round wafers about 6 inches in diameter before cooking; they come ready prepared and some stores carry different kinds — spicy, colored and plain.

To cook them: bake in a hot oven (400°F) for 3—4 minutes or until puffed, brown and crisp. Alternatively, fry them in hot deep oil (375°F on a fat thermometer), holding them down with a spatula for 10 seconds or until puffed and crisp, then drain on paper towels.

Note: ghee is Indian clarified butter (see box on page 83). Many Indians cook with vegetable oil and this can be substituted for ghee in all recipes.

Puris

Puris are chapatis that are deep fried instead of baked.

To make 9—10 puris: make and shape dough as for chapatis into 8—9 inch rounds. Heat a pan of deep oil to 350°F on a fat thermometer, lower in a puri and keep it immersed in oil with a slotted metal spatula so the puri puffs evenly all over. After about 30 seconds, turn it over and continue frying until both sides are golden brown. Drain on paper towels and keep warm while frying remaining puris.

Phulkas

Phulkas are small chapatis that are baked on small 5 inch tawas, then grilled on open coals until they puff.

To make 16—18 phulkas: divide chapati dough into balls and roll out to 5 inches in diameter. Bake as for chapatis, then broil them 6—7 inches from the heat until they puff up in patches. Serve at once.

Parathas

Paratha is wheat bread, layered with ghee, then fried.

To make 4—5 parathas: make dough as for chapatis and shape it into a long roll about 1 inch in diameter. Cut into 1 inch lengths and flatten or roll each piece to a 2—3 inch circle. Brush each circle with melted ghee and pile them one on top of the other, using 4—6 rounds for each cake and leaving the top one ungreased. With a rolling pin roll out the cakes to 9—10 inches diameter. Cover with a dampened towel until ready to fry. The parathas may be shaped up to 4 hours in advance.

To fry: heat a tablespoon of ghee in a large skillet and fry a paratha for 2 minutes over medium heat.
Watchpoint: do not let the paratha brown or it will be tough and hard.

Turn it, fry on the other side, turn again and fry 1 minute longer. All the ghee will be absorbed and the paratha should be crisp and flaky. Cover it with a cloth to keep warm while frying the remaining parathas.

SWEET DISHES

In India the art of making candies is usually a family tradition. These 'halvais' sell their confections in bazaars and small shops. Sweet dishes and candies are usually snacks, eaten between meals.

Firni
(Rice Cream with Pistachios)

2½ cups milk
3 tablespoons cream of rice
¼ teaspoon cardamom seed, crushed
1½ tablespoons sugar
¾ cup coconut milk
12 shelled pistachio nuts, blanched, peeled and coarsely chopped

Method
Scald the milk and, stirring constantly, slowly sprinkle in the cream of rice. Continue stirring until the mixture thickens to the consistency of heavy cream, then add the cardamom, sugar and coconut milk. Continue simmering 12—15 minutes or until the mixture is thick but still pours easily.

Pour into a bowl and cool. Sprinkle with pistachio nuts before serving cold.

> **Farina,** used in rasgulla, is a cream-colored granular cereal made from a hard durum wheat, and has a very low gluten content. It is often used as a breakfast cereal.

Rava

1½ tablespoons cream of rice
2½ cups milk
1 can (14 oz) condensed milk
1½ tablespoons sugar
2 egg yolks
1 tablespoon ghee
¼ cup shredded almonds
¼ cup raisins
2 teaspoons rose water
pinch of ground nutmeg

Method
Stir half the milk into the cream of rice and heat, stirring, until the mixture boils. Simmer gently to the consistency of heavy cream, stirring constantly. Stir the remaining milk into the condensed milk and sugar and add to the cream of rice mixture. Simmer again for 10—12 minutes or until the mixture is thick but still pours from a spoon. Take from the heat, beat in the egg yolks, then let cool.

Heat the ghee and lightly brown the almonds. Stir in the raisins, cook 1 minute until plump and drain on paper towels. Stir the rose water into the cream of rice and pour into a serving bowl. Sprinkle with raisins and almonds and a little nutmeg. Serve cold.

Rasgulla
(Cheese Balls in Syrup)

5 cups milk
juice of 2 lemons
¼ teaspoon cardamom seed, crushed
1 tablespoon farina (see box)
2 cups sugar
1¼ cups water
1 tablespoon rose water

Method
Scald the milk, take from heat and stir in lemon juice. Cover and let stand in a warm place until milk separates, then let cool. Lay a piece of cheesecloth over a bowl, pour in milk, lift up cheesecloth and tie it so whey can drain. Leave overnight so curd in the cheesecloth is fairly firm and dry.

Add cardamom seed and farina to the curd; work until smooth. Dissolve sugar in the water in a shallow pan over low heat, bring to a boil and cook until syrup forms a thread when a little is lifted on a spoon (230°F—234°F on a sugar thermometer).

Press curd mixture into walnut-sized balls and drop them gently into the simmering syrup. Simmer 15—20 minutes or until balls are puffy. Carefully lift out balls, arrange them in a serving dish and sprinkle with rose water. Serve warm at room temperature with the syrup.

Meeta Pilau
(Sweet Saffron Rice)

1 cup round grain rice
3 tablespoons ghee
pinch of salt
¼ cup cardamom seeds, crushed
¼ teaspoon ground cloves
¼ teaspoon ground cinnamon
about 1½ cups milk
¼ cup sugar
½ cup raisins
large pinch of saffron infused in 1 tablespoon hot milk for 30 minutes
¼ cup slivered almonds

Method
Cook the rice in plenty of boiling salted water for 6 minutes and drain it thoroughly. In a heavy saucepan heat the ghee and fry the rice gently, stirring, for 2—3 min-utes until all the ghee is absorbed. Add the salt, spices, milk and sugar and simmer 20—25 minutes or until the rice is tender and all the milk is absorbed. If the mixture gets dry before the rice is cooked, add a little more milk.

Watchpoint: use a non-stick or heavy-based pan so the rice does not scorch.

Stir the raisins and saffron milk into the rice with a fork — the texture should be creamy. Serve hot with the almonds sprinkled on top.

Jelabis

3 cups flour
pinch of salt
2 pinches of saffron, infused in ¾ cup boiling water for 30 minutes
1 package dry or 1 cake compressed yeast
½ cup yogurt
oil (for deep frying)

For syrup
3 cups sugar
1½ cups water
2—3 thin strips of lemon rind
juice of 1 lemon
2 tablespoons rose water
yellow food coloring

For decoration
½ cup shelled pistachios, coarsely chopped
½ cup fresh rose petals

Pastry bag; ¼ inch plain tube

Makes 22—24 jelabis.

Method
To make the dough: sift the flour and salt into a bowl, make a well in the center and add the saffron liquid, cooled to lukewarm. Sprinkle over the yeast and let stand 5 minutes until dissolved. Add the yogurt and work in the flour

Jelabis are garnished with rose petals and chopped pistachios

with the hand to form a smooth batter. Knead 5 minutes or until elastic. Cover the bowl and let stand in a warm place 1 hour or until light and full of bubbles.

To make syrup: heat the sugar with the water until dissolved, add the lemon rind and boil steadily until the syrup forms a thread when a little is lifted on a spoon (230°F–234°F on a sugar thermometer). Strain, add the lemon juice and cool. Then add the rose water and a few drops of yellow food coloring.

Heat the deep oil to 375°F on a fat thermometer.

Fill dough into the pastry bag fitted with the plain tube and squeeze dough into the oil in double circles like a figure 8. Fry until the jelabis are puffed and brown, drain on paper towels and drop them, while still hot, into the sugar syrup.

Leave 1–2 minutes, then lift out, drain off excess syrup and pile on a platter. Continue frying jelabis until all batter is used. Serve within 3–4 hours; sprinkle with pistachios and rose petals just before serving.

A FESTIVE BUFFET

Welcome guests with a mouth-watering, festive buffet. You can make both the fillet of beef, garnished with olives and eggplant, and the special chicken salad or take your choice of each and double the quantities to serve 12 people. Gâteau Margot, a light sponge cake, is layered with strawberry purée and chocolate for the dessert.

A diverse array of cold dishes calls for a wine that may be served cool and the ideal accompaniment is a good dry rosé. It is widely agreed that the world's best dry rosés come from Tavel in France's Rhône Valley. The best American alternative, made from the same grape, is the Grenache Rosé marketed by several California growers.

Fillet of Beef Niçoise
Hot Anchovy Loaf
Chicken Salad Milanaise

Avocado Mousse
Eggs Indochine
Lima Bean Salad

Gâteau Margot

Rosé Wine — Tavel (Rhône)
or Grenache (California)

The buffet menu for 12 includes (from left): avocado mousse, chicken salad Milanaise (in front), fillet of beef Niçoise and sour cream dressing, eggs Indochine and gâteau Margot filled with fresh strawberries

Make stock, mayonnaise and vinaigrette dressing. Make aspic for beef Niçoise. Make sponge cake for gâteau Margot and store in airtight container.

Day before
Roast beef and chicken. Hard-cook eggs for eggs Indochine and beef Niçoise. Make the curry mixture for eggs Indochine; halve eggs, make filling and keep in refrigerator in covered bowl. Keep egg whites in bowl of cold water at room temperature.
Prepare green peppers and olives for avocado mousse and beef Niçoise; cover olives with oil and keep at room temperature. Prepare tomatoes for beef Niçoise; store, covered, in refrigerator. Prepare lima bean salad but do not add dressing; keep tightly covered in refrigerator.

Morning
Wash watercress in cold water, wrap loosely in a damp towel; store in refrigerator vegetable drawer.
Slice sponge cake and brush with chocolate; prepare strawberry purée.
Prepare eggplant for beef Niçoise; complete garnish and store, covered. Slice beef, arrange on platter and coat with aspic; store in refrigerator. Make sour cream dressing, put in sauce boat and store, covered, in refrigerator.
Cook macaroni and mushrooms for chicken salad Milanaise. Cut ham and tongue in julienne strips;

carve chicken and store, covered, in refrigerator.
Prepare, but do not bake, anchovy loaf. Make avocado mousse, cover tightly with plastic wrap and chill. Mix garnish for mousse and keep, covered, in a bowl.
Prepare cucumber for eggs Indochine; fill hard-cooked eggs. Mix shrimps and cucumber with dressing, cover and chill.

Afternoon
Finish gâteau Margot and store in refrigerator.
Finish chicken salad Milanaise but do not add watercress; cover tightly with plastic wrap and store in refrigerator. Arrange eggs and salad on platter for eggs Indochine, but do not coat eggs; cover tightly with plastic wrap and store in refrigerator.
Pile Niçoise salad on beef platter, cover with plastic wrap; store in refrigerator.

Just before serving
Unmold mousse and garnish it.
Garnish chicken salad Milanaise with watercress.
Bake anchovy loaf and keep hot.
Make curry mayonnaise and coat eggs Indochine.
Toss lima bean salad with dressing.

You will find that **cooking times** given in the individual recipes for these dishes have sometimes been adapted in the timetable to help you when cooking and serving this menu as a party meal.

Fillet of Beef Niçoise

2½—3 lb fillet of beef
3 tablespoons olive oil (for roasting)
2 cups cool but still liquid aspic (see page 106)
hot anchovy loaf (to serve) — see page 104

For salad
1 eggplant
salt and pepper
6 tablespoons olive oil
1 onion, sliced
2 green peppers, cored, seeded, cut in strips and blanched
4 medium tomatoes, peeled, quartered and seeds removed
2—3 tablespoons vinaigrette dressing (see page 61)

For sour cream dressing
1 cup sour cream
1 clove of garlic, crushed
1 teaspoon paprika
black pepper, freshly ground
3 teaspoons lemon juice or wine vinegar, or to taste

For garnish
3 hard-cooked eggs, quartered
½ cup ripe olives, pitted

Serves 6—8 people.

Method
To roast the fillet of beef: in a roasting pan heat the olive oil, set the beef on a rack, baste it and roast in a hot oven (400°F) for $\frac{3}{4}$—1 hour for rare beef, or until a meat thermometer inserted in the beef registers 140°F. Take the pan from the oven and let the beef cool to room temperature in it.

To prepare salad: cut the eggplant in half lengthwise, cut each half into $\frac{1}{2}$ inch slices, sprinkle with salt and let stand 20—30 minutes to draw out the juices (dégorger). Rinse and dry with paper towels.

In a large skillet heat the olive oil and fry eggplant slices until lightly browned on both sides. Take out, lower the heat, add onion slices and continue cooking until onion is soft but not brown. Replace the eggplant, cover the pan and cook until the eggplant is tender. Add the green pepper, tomatoes and seasoning. Increase the heat and cook briskly for 1 minute. Transfer the vegetables to a bowl, let cool, then mix with the vinaigrette dressing.

To make sour cream dressing: beat the crushed garlic and paprika into the sour cream, season with pepper, add the lemon juice or wine vinegar to taste and pour into a sauce boat.

Carve the beef into three-eighth to half-inch slices and arrange them, overlapping, down one side of a platter. Chill thoroughly, brush the slices with cool but still liquid aspic, giving them 2—3 coatings and chill between each coating until aspic has set.

To serve: spoon the salad down the other side of the platter and garnish with hard-cooked egg and ripe olives. Serve sour cream dressing and hot anchovy loaf separately.

For the salad for fillet of beef Niçoise, fry eggplant and onion lightly in oil before adding peppers and tomatoes

Brush the cold beef slices with cool but still liquid aspic, letting each coating set before brushing them again

Add a luxury touch to your buffet with fillet of beef Niçoise

Hot Anchovy Loaf

Set oven at hot (425°F). Soak 6 anchovy fillets in a little milk for 10–15 minutes; drain and chop finely. Pound anchovies with $\frac{1}{2}$ cup unsalted butter; stir in a few drops of red food coloring — enough to make the butter pink. Season with plenty of black pepper, freshly ground.

Slice a loaf of French bread down to within $\frac{1}{2}$ inch of the crust. Spread anchovy butter between slices and on top and sides of the loaf. Wrap in foil and bake in heated oven for 10 minutes. Reduce oven heat to 400°F, open foil and bake 5–8 minutes longer or until crisp and brown. Remove foil and serve.

Chicken Salad Milanaise

3$\frac{1}{2}$–4 lb roasting chicken
$\frac{1}{4}$ cup butter
pinch of marjoram
salt and pepper
$\frac{1}{2}$ cup vermouth
1$\frac{1}{2}$ cups well-flavored chicken stock
$\frac{1}{2}$ lb cooked ham
$\frac{1}{2}$ lb cooked tongue
bunch of watercress (for garnish)

For salad
1 package (8 oz) small macaroni
3 cups ($\frac{3}{4}$ lb) mushrooms, thickly sliced
squeeze of lemon juice
3 tablespoons olive oil
1 cup mayonnaise (see page 11)

Serves 6–8 people.

Method
Set oven at hot (400°F).

Put 1 tablespoon of the butter with a pinch of marjoram and seasoning inside the chicken, truss neatly and rub the remaining butter over the skin. Put the bird in a roasting pan, pour around the vermouth, lightly cover bird with a piece of foil and roast in heated oven for 1$\frac{1}{4}$–1$\frac{1}{2}$ hours or until no pink juice runs out when the chicken is pierced in the thigh with a skewer. After 20 minutes, baste the bird, and turn it on its side. Continue basting and turning the bird every 20 minutes, ending with the breast up. Remove the foil for the last 15 minutes cooking. When the vermouth has evaporated and the butter begins to brown, add a little of the chicken stock.

Remove the chicken from the roasting pan and let stand until cool. Pour the remaining stock into the pan, bring to a boil, scraping to dissolve the sediment; strain and chill.

To prepare salad: cook the macaroni in boiling salted water for about 10–12 minutes or until 'al dente'. Then drain and rinse thoroughly under cold water. Put mushrooms in a buttered pan with the lemon juice, press a piece of buttered foil on top and cook over high heat for 1 minute or until just tender; leave on a plate to cool. Toss mushrooms with oil until thoroughly coated and add seasoning.

Carve the chicken, cutting the meat into neat, even-sized pieces, discarding bones and skin.

Cut the ham and the tongue into julienne strips.

Remove all traces of fat from the cold chicken gravy and strain it. Mix it with the strips of ham and tongue.

Watchpoint: ham loses its pink color if exposed to air, so if it is cut into julienne strips some time before using, store it in a bowl and cover tightly with plastic wrap.

To serve: mix mayonnaise with macaroni and mushrooms, taste for seasoning and pile in a serving dish. Arrange chicken pieces on top. Put the ham and tongue strips on top of the chicken and garnish the dish with watercress.

Avocado Mousse

2–3 ripe avocados
1 envelope gelatin
$\frac{1}{2}$ cup cold water
$\frac{1}{2}$ cup boiling water or chicken stock
1 teaspoon onion juice
2 teaspoons Worcestershire sauce
salt and pepper
$\frac{3}{4}$ cup mayonnaise (see page 11)
$\frac{1}{2}$ cup heavy cream, whipped until it holds a soft shape

For garnish
2 tablespoons vinaigrette dressing (see page 61)
2 green peppers, cored, seeded, cut in strips and blanched
$\frac{1}{3}$ cup ripe olives, halved and pitted

Ring mold (5 cup capacity)

Serves 6–8 people.

Method
Lightly oil the ring mold. Sprinkle the gelatin over the cold water and let stand for 5 minutes until soft. Pour in the boiling water or stock and stir until dissolved. Peel and halve the avocados, discard the seeds and crush the fruit with a fork (there should be 1$\frac{1}{2}$ cups crushed avocado). Stir gelatin into avocado with onion juice, Worcestershire sauce and a little salt and pepper. When the mixture is cold, fold in mayonnaise and lightly whipped cream. Season to taste and pour into the prepared mold; seal tightly with plastic wrap and chill 1–2 hours or until set.

Watchpoint: seal mold well to prevent discoloring.

To prepare garnish: mix the vinaigrette dressing with the peppers and olives. Just before serving, turn mousse out onto a platter; pile garnish into center and around edge.

A tempting buffet includes, clockwise from right: eggs Indochine, chicken salad Milanaise, avocado mousse and fillet of beef Niçoise

Eggs Indochine

8 hard-cooked eggs
½ cup butter, softened
1 teaspoon tomato paste

For salad
2 cucumbers
salt
1 tablespoon olive oil
½ teaspoon sugar
black pepper, freshly ground
1 teaspoon white wine vinegar
½ lb cooked, peeled medium
    shrimps
2 teaspoons chopped parsley
    or mint

For curry mayonnaise
2 teaspoons curry powder
1¼ cups mayonnaise
    (see page 11)
1 tablespoon chopped onion
1 clove of garlic, crushed
2 tablespoons oil
¾ cup tomato juice
1 slice of lemon
1 tablespoon apricot jam
pepper
squeeze of lemon juice
    (optional)

Serves 6–8 people.

Method
To make the curry mixture: cook the onion and garlic in the oil until soft but not brown, stir in curry powder and continue cooking for 1 minute. Pour in tomato juice, add the slice of lemon and simmer 7–10 minutes. Add apricot jam, bring the mixture to a boil, strain and cool.

To prepare the salad: peel cucumbers and cut them in julienne strips, discarding the seeds. Sprinkle with 1 teaspoon salt, cover and let stand about 30 minutes to draw out the juices (dégorger). Rinse with cold water and dry with paper towels. Toss cucumber gently in the oil until the strips are coated. Season with sugar and pepper, sprinkle with vinegar and mix again. Combine the cucumber mixture with the shrimps and parsley or mint and taste for seasoning.

Cut the hard-cooked eggs in half, remove the yolks and work them through a strainer into a bowl. Mix in the softened butter, tomato paste and about 1 teaspoon of the curry mixture. Wash and dry the egg whites, fill them with the mixture and put 2 halves together to reshape the eggs. Arrange the eggs in a semi-circle on a platter.

To make the curry mayonnaise: stir remaining curry mixture into the mayonnaise, taste for seasoning and add a squeeze of lemon juice, if you like.

Coat the eggs with about half the curry mayonnaise, pile the cucumber and shrimp salad in the center of the platter and serve remaining curry mayonnaise separately.

Lima Bean Salad

3 cups fresh shelled lima beans
    or 2 packages frozen lima
    beans
3–4 stalks of celery, sliced
1 small dill pickle, sliced
6 tablespoons vinaigrette
    dressing (see page 61)
1 tablespoon chopped chives

Method
Cook the beans in boiling salted water for 15–20 minutes or until just tender or cook frozen lima beans according to package directions; drain, refresh and drain again.

Mix the beans with the celery and dill pickle, pile in a salad bowl, spoon over the vinaigrette dressing, and sprinkle with chives.

Aspic

2 envelopes gelatin
¼ cup sherry
¼ cup white wine
3½ cups cold brown stock
1 teaspoon wine vinegar
2 egg whites

The amount of gelatin given in this recipe will set a liquid or very lightly jellied stock firmly enough to turn out of a mold.

Method
Sprinkle gelatin over sherry and wine in a small pan and leave 5 minutes until spongy. Pour the cold stock into a scalded pan or kettle and add the vinegar. Whisk the egg whites to a froth, add them to the pan, set it over moderate heat and whisk backwards until the stock is hot. Add the gelatin, and continue whisking steadily until the mixture boils.

Stop whisking and let the liquid rise to the top of the pan; turn off the heat or draw the pan aside and leave to settle for about 5 minutes. Bring to a boil again, draw the pan aside once more and leave the liquid to settle. At this point the liquid seen through the egg white filter should look clear. If not, repeat the boiling process.

Filter the aspic through a cloth or jelly bag and cool before using.

For eggs Indochine, cut cucumbers into julienne strips, discarding seeds

Rich gâteau Margot is layered with a cream and strawberry purée mixture

Gâteau Margot

1½ cups cake flour
pinch of salt
6 eggs
1½ cups sugar

For filling
2 boxes fresh strawberries, hulled, or 2 packages frozen strawberries without sugar, thawed
5–6 tablespoons sugar
8 squares (8 oz) semisweet chocolate
2 cups heavy cream, stiffly whipped
1 teaspoon vanilla

Two 9 inch tube pans or ring mold (2 quart capacity each)

This recipe makes 2 cakes to serve 12 people.

Method

Set oven at moderately hot (375°F). Grease the tube pans or ring mold, sprinkle with sugar, then with flour and discard the excess.

Sift flour 2–3 times with the salt.

Break the eggs into a large bowl and gradually beat in the sugar. Set the bowl over a pan of boiling water — the bowl should not touch the water — take the pan from the heat and beat the sugar and eggs for 10–12 minutes or until the mixture is light and thick enough to leave a ribbon trail on itself when the beater is lifted. Remove bowl from the pan and continue beating until the mixture is cold (3–4 minutes longer). If using an electric beater, no heat is necessary.

With a metal spoon, cut and fold the flour into the mixture. Divide the batter into the pans and bake in the heated oven for 25–30 minutes or until the cakes spring back when lightly pressed with a

fingertip. Cool cakes in the pan for a few minutes, then turn out onto a wire rack to cool completely.

Cut about one-third of the strawberries into thick slices, sprinkle them with 1 tablespoon of the sugar and let stand for 10–15 minutes. Work them through a sieve or in a blender to make a purée.

Chop the chocolate and melt it on a heatproof plate over a pan of hot water. Cut the cakes across into 3 layers, spread the bottom and middle layers with a thin coating of chocolate and let stand until set.

Fold about one-third of the stiffly whipped cream into the strawberry purée; spread this over these 4 layers and re-shape the cakes. Flavor remaining whipped cream with remaining sugar to taste, and the vanilla and spread over each cake; pile the remaining strawberries in the center.

▲
Spread whipped cream and strawberry purée mixture on cooled layers of chocolate

Reshape the gâteau Margot and spread all over with remaining whipped cream flavored with sugar and vanilla
▼

HOW TO MAKE CANDIES

Candies are fun to make and even more fun to give away because they are ideal for colorful gift wrappings of tissue paper and ribbon.

Most candies are not hard to make but you must pay close attention to be sure that they are cooked and worked to exactly the right stage. Unless you are an experienced candy-maker, a sugar thermometer is almost indispensable when boiling.

It is easier to make a fairly large batch of candy at one time because small quantities of ingredients are hard to measure accurately, but you can often make a variety of candies from a basic mixture by adding different colorings and flavors.

Candies shown at left in colorful wrappings include molasses toffee and marzipan walnuts at the top with peppermint creams in the center. In boxes are rows of coffee nut fudge, white coconut ice, marzipan walnuts, molasses toffee, pink coconut ice, chocolate fudge and marzipan dates

Stages and Tests for Boiling Sugar Syrup

Stage	Temperature on Sugar Thermometer	Test
Thread	230°F–234°F	Long thread forms when syrup is tested between finger and thumb
Soft Ball	240°F	Syrup forms a soft ball when dropped in cold water
Hard Ball	250°F	Syrup forms a firm, pliable ball when dropped in cold water
Light Crack	268°F	Syrup forms a solid ball when dropped in cold water
Medium Crack	275°F	Syrup forms a brittle ball when dropped in cold water
Hard Crack	289°F–292°F	Syrup forms a tear drop shape when dropped in cold water
Extra Hard Crack	300°F	Syrup forms a brittle thread when dropped in cold water
Caramelized	310°F–338°F	Syrup looks pale golden

To test sugar syrup for the thread stage (230°F–234°F on sugar thermometer): cool a little on a spoon and when cool pull between your finger and thumb into a fine thread

Points to remember

1 Choose a large saucepan, because boiling sugar rises in the pan. It should have a heavy base to distribute heat evenly.
2 Once the sugar has completely dissolved, boil mixture steadily so that it cooks evenly.
3 Never stir boiling sugar unless instructions say so.
4 Use the best ingredients – the small extra cost is amply justified by the improved flavor of the candies. Fresh cream and milk are best for mixtures where long cooking at a high temperature is involved. However, in some recipes, evaporated and condensed milk are preferred; e.g., when added after cooking is completed.

5 Humidity is the enemy of candy-makers; try to make candies in a cool, dry kitchen and make only 1–2 batches at one time so that the humidity does not build up.
6 Candies are best eaten fresh although most can be kept for 1–2 weeks in airtight containers. Pack them in fancy wrappings at the last possible moment; when exposed to air, many candies such as taffy become sticky, while others like fudge tend to dry and harden on the outside.

Candy-making Equipment

Heavy saucepans of stainless steel, aluminum or tin-lined copper are best. Do not use enameled iron as the continual boiling of syrups to high temperatures may damage the enamel. Two pans (1 quart and 2 quart capacities) should be sufficient.
Sugar thermometer should be clearly marked and register up to 400°F. A movable clip that attaches to side of saucepan makes it easy to take an accurate reading. Test the thermometer by heating it slowly in a pan of water. When boiling, it should read 212°F. Allow it to cool in the water.
Wooden spoons are best.
Pastry brush should be used (wet) to dissolve mixture that crystallizes on pan sides so no crystals slide back down into rest of mixture. Pan sides should be kept very clean.

Use and Care of Sugar Thermometer

Stand thermometer in hot water before and after immersing in boiling liquid. Always lower the thermometer gently into the liquid and check that the bulb is covered, or the reading will be inaccurate. Stoop down to read so that your eye is level with the thermometer. Wash and dry the thermometer and store it carefully.

Coconut Ice

2 cans (4 oz each) unsweetened
  shredded coconut
4 cups sugar
1½ cups milk
½ teaspoon vanilla
red food coloring

8 inch square cake pan

Makes 1¼ lb.

Method

Lightly oil the pan.

In a large, heavy-based pan put sugar and milk and heat, stirring, until sugar has dissolved. Bring mixture to a boil and cook steadily, without stirring, for 10 minutes to the soft ball stage (240°F on a sugar thermometer). Take from heat, let bubbles subside and stir in the coconut and vanilla.

Pour one-half of the mixture into the prepared pan. Color the remainder of the mixture a delicate pink with red food coloring and pour carefully on top of the white mixture. Mark into ¾ inch X 1½ inch bars before mixture is quite cold.

Wrap in wax paper and store in an airtight container.

Molasses Toffee

½ cup molasses
2 cups dark brown sugar
½ cup light corn syrup
small can (6 oz) condensed
  milk
¼ cup butter
1 tablespoon vinegar
1 teaspoon vanilla

8 inch square cake pan

Makes about 1¾ lb.

Method

Butter the cake pan.

In a large heavy-based pan put all ingredients except vanilla and stir over gentle heat until the sugar has dissolved. Bring to a boil and cook steadily, stirring constantly, for 15–20 minutes or to the extra hard crack stage (300°F on a sugar thermometer).

Take from heat, add vanilla and pour into the prepared pan. When almost cold, mark deeply with a knife into squares. When completely cold turn out and tap the back with the handle of a knife — the toffee should snap apart into squares. Wrap each one neatly in wax paper or foil and keep in an airtight container.

Coffee Nut Fudge

2 tablespoons dry instant
  coffee
1 cup browned and coarsely
  chopped almonds
1 cup coarsely chopped
  walnuts
½ cup unsalted butter
1½ cups milk
2 cups sugar
1 teaspoon vanilla

8 inch square cake pan

Makes 2 lb.

Method

Grease the cake pan. In a large heavy-based pan melt butter, add milk, sugar and coffee and stir gently over low heat until the sugar has dissolved. Bring to a boil and continue cooking 15–20 minutes, stirring constantly, to the soft ball stage (240°F on a sugar thermometer).

Take from heat and cool until lukewarm (110°F on a sugar thermometer) without stirring.

Watchpoint: fudge will be grainy if stirred while too hot.

Beat fudge until it is stiff and no longer shiny. Beat in almonds and walnuts with the vanilla and spread in the prepared pan. Mark into squares before the fudge is quite cold.

Wrap squares in wax paper and store in an airtight container.

Chocolate Fudge

3 squares (3 oz) unsweetened
  chocolate
3 cups sugar
1 envelope gelatin
1 cup milk
½ cup light corn syrup
1¼ cups butter
1 cup chopped pecans
2 teaspoons vanilla

9 inch square cake pan

Makes 1½ lb.

Method

Grease cake pan. Put sugar and dry gelatin in a heavy-based pan with the milk, corn syrup, chocolate and butter and cook over medium heat, stirring occasionally, until it reaches the soft ball stage (240°F on a sugar thermometer). Complete and store as for coffee nut fudge.

Peppermint Creams

2–3 drops oil of peppermint,
  or ¼ teaspoon peppermint
  extract
3½ cups (1 lb) confectioners'
  sugar
1 egg white
1–1½ tablespoons water
extra confectioners' sugar,
  sifted (for shaping)

*1½ inch round cookie cutter,
  or small wineglass*

Makes 45–50 creams. Oil of peppermint is available at pharmacies.

Method

Sift confectioners' sugar into a bowl. Beat the egg white until it holds a soft peak and stir into the sugar with the water. Work mixture until it forms a smooth paste. Flavor carefully with oil of peppermint (it is very strong) or with peppermint extract.

Sprinkle a board generously with sifted confectioners' sugar and knead the peppermint mixture on it until smooth, adding more sugar if necessary. Roll it out to ¼–½ inch thickness and cut into rounds with a cutter or wineglass. Place on wax paper and leave overnight to dry. Store them in an airtight container.

Put taffy into attractive jars to make a pleasing gift

White Taffy

2 cups sugar
$\frac{2}{3}$ cup water
$\frac{2}{3}$ cup light corn syrup
2 tablespoons butter
1 teaspoon vanilla

Makes about $1\frac{3}{4}$ lb.

Method

Lightly oil a marble slab or baking sheet.

In a large heavy-based pan put sugar, water and corn syrup and heat gently until sugar has dissolved. Bring to a boil and cook steadily, without stirring, to the hard ball stage (250°F on a sugar thermometer). Add butter and continue boiling until mixture reaches the light crack stage (268°F on a sugar thermometer). Pour onto the prepared marble slab or baking sheet.

When mixture is cool enough to handle, pour vanilla into the center of the mixture, oil your hands and pull sides of mixture into the center to work in the vanilla. Continue working and pulling the mixture until it is opaque and very stiff. Pull it into long ropes about $\frac{3}{4}$ inch in diameter and cut them into $1-1\frac{1}{2}$ inch pieces with scissors. Layer with wax paper, if you like, and store in an airtight container.

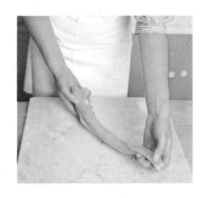

Pull the taffy mixture until it is opaque and very stiff

Cut the long taffy ropes into small pieces with scissors

Striped Taffy

Divide a batch of taffy in half or into thirds; add vanilla and leave one portion white. Color the second portion yellow or pink and the third green. Work portions as for white taffy until fairly stiff, then join the ends together and work into ropes, twisting to braid the colors.

Peppermint Cushions

Flavor the taffy with 2–3 drops of oil of peppermint instead of the vanilla and work as for white taffy until fairly stiff. Pull into ropes, cut into 2 inch lengths with scissors and fold each piece in half to form a cushion shape.
Note: oil of peppermint is available at pharmacies.

Molasses Taffy

2 cups molasses
1 cup granulated sugar
1 cup dark brown sugar
$\frac{3}{4}$ cup water
$\frac{1}{4}$ cup butter
$\frac{1}{4}$ teaspoon baking soda
$\frac{1}{4}$ teaspoon salt

Makes about 2 lb.

Method

Lightly oil a marble slab or baking sheet.

In a large heavy-based pan put both kinds of sugar, molasses and water and heat gently until sugar has dissolved. Bring to a boil and cook steadily, without stirring, to the light crack stage (268°F on a sugar thermometer). Take from heat, add butter, soda and salt and stir just enough to mix well; the mixture will foam slightly when the soda is added.

Pour onto the prepared marble slab or baking sheet and leave until the mixture is cool enough to handle. Pull, cut in pieces and store as for white taffy.

Maple Divinity

$\frac{1}{2}$ cup maple syrup
$2\frac{1}{3}$ cups sugar
$\frac{2}{3}$ cup light corn syrup
$\frac{1}{4}$ teaspoon salt
$\frac{1}{4}$ cup water
2 egg whites
1 cup coarsely chopped walnuts or pecans
$\frac{1}{2}$ teaspoon vanilla

Makes 36–40 candies.

Method

Put maple syrup, sugar, corn syrup, salt and water into a large, heavy-based pan and heat gently until sugar has dissolved. Bring to a boil and cook steadily, without stirring, to the light crack stage (268°F on a sugar thermometer).

While the syrup boils, beat egg whites until they hold a stiff peak. As soon as the syrup is ready, pour it onto the egg whites, beating constantly. Continue beating until mixture is cool and stiff. Stir in the nuts and vanilla. On a piece of wax paper, shape the mixture into $1\frac{1}{2}$ inch mounds with 2 teaspoons. When cold, layer with wax paper and store in an airtight container.
Watchpoint: shape the divinity quickly or it will set.

Serve a selection of glacé fruits in individual paper cases

Glacé Fruits

black and green grapes
orange or tangerine sections
fresh strawberries
fresh cherries, stems left on

For syrup
$\frac{1}{2}$ cup sugar
$\frac{1}{4}$ cup water
2 tablespoons light corn syrup,
    or pinch of cream of tartar,
    dissolved in a little water

Paper candy cases

These attractive colorful fruits can also be served as petits fours. To be at their best, glacé fruits should be eaten within 1–2 hours. This quantity of syrup is enough to coat 1 pint of strawberries or cherries, or 1 small bunch of grapes, or the equivalent amount of tangerine or orange sections.

Method
Oil a baking sheet or large plate. Pick over fruit, making sure it is ripe and quite dry.

In a small, heavy-based pan over gentle heat, dissolve sugar in water together with corn syrup, or dissolved cream of tartar, bring to a boil and boil rapidly to the extra hard crack stage (300°F on a sugar thermometer). Stop the cooking by dipping bottom of pan in cold water. As soon as bubbles have subsided, dip each fruit in separately, holding the stem, or use a two-pronged fork or skewer.

Place fruit at once on the prepared sheet or plate and leave to set.

Each fruit should be completely coated in syrup with little or none forming a pool around the base. When syrup is hard, place fruits in individual paper cases.

Hold the cherries by the stem when dipping them into syrup

Marzipan Candies

3 cups whole almonds,
    blanched and ground
2 cups granulated sugar
1 cup water
2 egg whites, lightly beaten
3–4 tablespoons confectioners'
    sugar

For coloring and flavoring
1 teaspoon vanilla
green food coloring
$\frac{1}{4}$ teaspoon almond extract,
    or 1–2 teaspoons rum
red and yellow food coloring
2 teaspoons grated orange rind
2 teaspoons orange juice
$\frac{1}{2}$ teaspoon dry instant coffee,
    dissolved in 1 teaspoon
    water

Method
In a saucepan heat sugar with water until dissolved. Bring to a boil and cook steadily, without stirring, until syrup spins a thread (230°F–234°F on a sugar thermometer). Take pan from heat and beat until syrup looks slightly cloudy. Stir in the ground almonds, add egg whites and cook over gentle heat for 2–3 minutes or until mixture pulls away from sides of pan. Turn mixture onto a board sprinkled with a little of the confectioners' sugar.

While mixture is still warm, knead until quite smooth, working in the rest of the confectioners' sugar. Divide into four and color and flavor as follows:
1 Leave one portion white and flavor with vanilla.
2 Color second portion green and flavor with almond extract or rum.
3 Color third portion orange (combining red and yellow colorings) and flavor with orange rind and juice.
4 Color and flavor the fourth portion with instant coffee.

The colors should be clear but not harsh; add more flavorings to taste and knead the marzipan until smooth.

Roll the marzipan into large olive shapes. If it becomes dry during rolling, work in a few drops of warm water. Wrap each candy in wax paper or foil; store in an airtight container.

Marzipan Dates

Remove pits from dessert dates by making a slit along one side and lifting out the pit with the point of a knife.

Roll marzipan with your hands into a tube about $\frac{1}{2}$ inch thick and cut off even-sized pieces with a knife. Shape into ovals, press a blanched whole almond in the middle and insert the marzipan into each date. Roll in granulated sugar and wrap and store as above.

Marzipan Walnuts

If you like, roll marzipan into walnut-sized balls and press a walnut half on each side; wrap and store as above.

Walnut Brittle

3 cups coarsely chopped black
    or English walnuts
1 teaspoon baking soda
1 teaspoon vanilla
3 cups sugar
1 cup water
$\frac{1}{2}$ cup molasses
$\frac{1}{2}$ cup light corn syrup
2 tablespoons butter
$\frac{1}{2}$ teaspoon salt

Makes $2\frac{1}{2}$ lb.

Method
Lightly oil a marble slab or 2 large baking sheets.

Mix the soda with the vanilla and place near the stove.

In a large heavy-based pan gently heat sugar with water, molasses and corn syrup until sugar has dissolved. Bring to a boil and cook steadily, without stirring, to the light crack stage (268°F on a sugar thermometer). Stir in the walnuts in a steady stream, add butter and salt and continue cooking, stirring constantly, to the extra hard crack stage (300°F on a sugar thermometer). Take pan from heat and at once stir in the vanilla and soda mixture. The candy will foam and look fluffy.

Stir until thoroughly mixed and pour at once onto the prepared baking sheets or marble slab.

Spread with a spoon until the brittle is $\frac{1}{4}$ inch thick. As soon as it is cool enough to handle, pull edges to stretch the brittle out as thinly as possible. When set and cold, break into 2–3 inch pieces, layer with wax paper and store the pieces in an airtight container.

Sugared Nuts

2½ cups pecan or walnut
    halves, or whole almonds
    (blanched and browned)
1½ cups sugar
½ cup water
½ cup light corn syrup
½ teaspoon salt
½ teaspoon vanilla

Makes 2 lb.

Method
Lightly oil 2 baking sheets.

In a large heavy-based pan, put sugar, water and corn syrup and heat gently until sugar has dissolved. Bring to a boil and cook steadily, without stirring, to the hard ball stage (250°F on a sugar thermometer). Take from the heat, stir in salt and vanilla and then the nuts.

Stir mixture until the nuts are thoroughly coated and the syrup starts to crystallize and looks opaque. Turn mixture onto the prepared baking sheets. Separate nuts as quickly as possible with 2 forks. If the syrup sets too quickly, set the baking sheet in a very low oven (175°F–200°F) for a few minutes until it softens again.

Let nuts stand until the coating dries, then store them between sheets of wax paper in an airtight container.

Orange Caramel Nuts

Follow the recipe for sugared nuts, but make the syrup with 2 cups brown sugar instead of 1½ cups granulated sugar. After taking pan from heat, add 1 tablespoon grated orange rind to the syrup with the salt and vanilla.

Spiced Nuts

Follow the recipe for sugared nuts and, after taking pan from heat, add 1½ teaspoons cinnamon and ½ teaspoon allspice to the syrup with the salt and vanilla.

Buttered Nuts

¼ cup walnut halves
8–12 shelled Brazil nuts
½ cup whole almonds, blanched
2 cups light brown sugar
½ cup water
¼ cup light corn syrup
½ cup unsalted butter
little melted butter

Makes about 1¼–1½ lb.

Method
Lightly oil a baking sheet.

In a large heavy-based pan put sugar, water and corn syrup and heat gently until sugar has dissolved. Add the butter, bring to a boil and brush the top area of the pan with the melted butter – this helps prevent mixture from boiling over. Cook steadily, stirring constantly, until the mixture reaches the medium crack stage (275°F on a sugar thermometer). Remove from heat.

When bubbles have subsided and mixture begins to cool, drop in 3–4 nuts. Lift them out one at a time with a spoon and place on the prepared baking sheet, turning the spoon so the butterscotch mixture coats the nuts evenly. Continue until all the nuts are coated. If mixture becomes hard before finishing, melt it over gentle heat but try not to cook it further.

Leave nuts until hard, then wrap each one in wax paper or foil and store them in an airtight container.

Nougat

1 cup sugar
½ cup water
3 tablespoons light corn syrup
2 egg whites
½ cup clear honey
2½ cups whole almonds,
    blanched, halved and
    browned
½ cup shelled pistachios
½ cup chopped candied fruits
    (optional)
1 teaspoon vanilla

8 X 12 inch cake pan

Makes about 1½ lb.

Method
Line the cake pan with wax paper.

In a large, heavy-based pan put sugar, water and half the corn syrup. Heat gently until sugar has dissolved. Bring to a boil and cook steadily, without stirring, to the hard crack stage (289°F–292°F on a sugar thermometer).

While syrup boils, beat egg whites until they hold a stiff peak. When syrup is ready, pour it onto the egg whites, beating constantly, and continue beating until cool.

Boil remaining corn syrup with the honey and cook steadily to the hard crack stage (289°F–292°F on a sugar thermometer). Add to the egg white and syrup mixture, beating constantly. Stir in the nuts and candied fruits, if used, and set the bowl over a pan of hot water. Heat, stirring, until the mixture dries – when it holds its shape when cold and is not sticky to the touch it is done.

Add vanilla and spoon into the prepared pan. Cover with wax paper, place a board or other smooth surface on the candy and leave 12–24 hours. Remove the paper and cut nougat into squares. Wrap each square in wax paper or foil and store them in an airtight container.

FONDANT CANDIES

Fondant is the foundation of most chocolate-covered creams and bonbons. The ingredients are simple – sugar, water, flavoring and a few drops of coloring to tint the mixture a delicate pastel shade. However, the correct meltingly smooth texture of fondant is hard to achieve and depends on cooking the sugar syrup to exactly the right temperature, then working it to the correct consistency.

Fondant is also quite frequently used for icing many European cakes and gâteaux because it is particularly glossy and soft.

Homemade fondant candies — Boston Kisses, opera fondants, Neapolitan fondants — are good with after-dinner coffee and liqueurs or instead of dessert

Equipment for Fondant

Marble slab. This is ideal for fondant because it cools the syrup quickly and evenly. However, a heavy heatproof tray or roasting pan can be used for cooling the syrup, then it should be turned onto a Formica-type surface to be worked. Do not pour hot syrup directly onto a Formica-type surface.

Sugar scraper is not essential but makes working the fondant much easier. It is a piece of metal about 4 X 3 inches with a wooden handle or with one side of the metal bent over to form the handle. A **metal spatula** and **wooden spoon** can be used instead.

Sugar thermometer is essential.

Rules for Sugar Boiling

1 Use the correct proportion of sugar and water with only enough water to dissolve the sugar easily. If too much water is added, the syrup will boil for too long and is more likely to crystallize slightly or 'grain'.

2 Do not let the liquid boil until all the sugar has dissolved.

3 While dissolving sugar, stir as follows: touch the bottom of the saucepan with a wooden spoon, then draw it gently through any crystals settling at the bottom of the pan. This way the syrup is stirred at its own level, not washed up the sides of the pan.

4 Wash any crystals from the sides of the pan back into the syrup with a clean pastry brush dipped in warm water.

5 Corn syrup or cream of tartar (dissolved in a small amount of water) added after the sugar dissolves helps prevent the syrup from 'graining'.

6 Skim syrup well, put in sugar thermometer and boil steadily.

7 Do not stir boiling syrup unless directed to do so.

8 Continue to brush down the sides of the pan during boiling.

9 When the correct temperature is reached, remove pan from the heat at once. Take out the thermometer and put it in a pitcher of hot water.

Candy Fondant

4 cups sugar
$1\frac{1}{2}$ cups water
3 tablespoons corn syrup, or
$\frac{1}{4}$ teaspoon cream of tartar (dissolved in 1 teaspoon water)

Makes about $1\frac{1}{2}$ lb candy.

Method
Place sugar and water in a large saucepan over low heat and dissolve sugar slowly, following the rules for sugar boiling. When dissolved, add the corn syrup or dissolved cream of tartar, bring to a boil and boil steadily to the soft ball stage (240°F on a sugar thermometer). Take pan at once from the heat, let bubbles subside and pour mixture slowly onto a dampened marble slab or into a dampened roasting pan.

Cool mixture slightly, then pull the batch together with a sugar scraper or metal spatula, taking the mixture from the edge to the center. Leave until the candy feels just warm to the touch. If using a roasting pan turn out onto a Formica-type surface. Work vigorously with a metal spatula or sugar scraper in one hand and a wooden spoon in the other, turning and pulling it to the center until it becomes white and creamy — it will do this very suddenly and will become too stiff to work. Then take a small piece of fondant at a time and work it with the fingers until smooth. Pack into a bowl or jar, cover tightly and leave at least 1 hour and preferably 2–3 days to mellow. Fondant can be kept for 3–4 weeks if tightly covered.

For candy fondant pull slightly cooled batch of fondant together with sugar scraper

Turn and work fondant with scraper and wooden spoon

Butter Fondant

Make as for candy fondant and add 2 tablespoons unsalted butter to mixture after cooling and just before working it.

Chocolate Fondant

Melt 3 squares (3 oz) unsweetened chocolate on a heatproof plate over a pan of hot water. Make candy fondant and, after cooling and just before working, add melted chocolate to mixture with 1 teaspoon vanilla, or dry instant coffee or rum.

To finish fondant: the consistency of finished fondant will vary from soft and pliable to stiff and almost hard, depending on the humidity of the atmosphere in the kitchen and the exact temperature to which fondant was boiled.

To shape fondant: if it is pliable after mellowing, it can be shaped at once. If it is very stiff, soften it in the top of a double boiler with 1–2 tablespoons of sugar syrup or water, stirring constantly; do not let it heat above lukewarm or it will lose its gloss. Then cool it and shape.

To color and flavor fondant: if coloring and flavoring a whole batch of candy, add coloring and flavoring after cooling and just before working the mixture. If dividing the batch, add coloring and flavoring when shaping.

Icing Fondant (for cakes)
Make as for candy fondant, but use $\frac{1}{4}$ cup corn syrup instead of 3 tablespoons and boil to 242°F on a sugar thermometer.

After working coconut into candy fondant for Boston kisses, color portions separately

Divide the fondant into walnut-sized pieces, shape into crescents, then leave them to harden

Boston Kisses

4 cup quantity candy fondant
$1\frac{1}{2}$ cups shredded coconut
3–4 tablespoons confectioners' sugar (for sprinkling)

For flavoring and coloring
vanilla (for white)
lemon extract with yellow food coloring (for yellow)
violet essence with blue and red food coloring (for lilac)
rose water with red food coloring (for pink)

Violet essence and rose water are available at pharmacies and specialty stores. Substitute a liqueur, or orange or lemon extract if you cannot find them. Makes about $1\frac{3}{4}$ lb candy.

Method
Work the coconut into the fondant, divide in four and color and flavor each quarter differently. Divide quarters into walnut-sized pieces, shape into crescents on a board or marble slab sprinkled with confectioners' sugar and leave overnight on a sheet of wax paper to harden. Pack in wax paper and store in an airtight container.

Neapolitan Fondants

2 cup quantity candy fondant, colored pink and flavored with rose water
2 cup quantity chocolate fondant or white fondant, colored violet and flavored with violet essence
3 cup quantity boiled marzipan
1 egg white, beaten until frothy

Makes about 3 lb candy.

Method
Roll out both kinds of fondant to rectangles $\frac{1}{4}$ inch thick on a board or marble slab sprinkled with confectioners' sugar, taking care to make rectangles the same size and thickness.

Make marzipan and roll out to the same size as fondant. Brush 1 portion of fondant thinly with egg white and place marzipan on top. Brush with more egg white and top with remaining fondant.

Cover fondant with wax paper and put a flat board or baking sheet with a light weight on top. The pressure should be even and just enough to press the layers without squeezing them. Leave 2–3 hours until set. Cut with a very sharp knife into rectangles. Pack in wax paper in an airtight container.

Opera Fondants

4 cup quantity of butter fondant
$\frac{3}{4}$ cup evaporated milk or heavy cream
3–4 cups sifted confectioners' sugar

Small fancy cutters

Makes about $1\frac{3}{4}$ lb candy.

Method
Melt fondant in the top of a double boiler over very gentle heat, beating constantly.

Watchpoint: the fondant must be beaten constantly at this point.

Take from the heat and stir in evaporated milk or cream. Beat in confectioners' sugar a spoonful at a time until the mixture is stiff enough to handle, then turn out onto a marble slab or board and divide in four. Color and flavor as for Boston Kisses and knead until very smooth. While still warm and pliable, roll out fondant to $\frac{1}{2}$ inch thickness, using confectioners' sugar to prevent sticking. Cut in shapes with small fancy cutters, place on a sheet of wax paper and leave to dry overnight. Pack in wax paper and store in an airtight container.

Crêpes Suzette (recipe is on page 130)

HOW TO MAKE CREPES (2)

From everyone's point of view, crêpes are a popular party dish; guests are delighted by the rich creamy fillings of savory crêpes or the sweet-tart taste of many crêpe desserts; hostesses appreciate the convenience of preparing crêpes in advance and the ease of providing such a luxurious dish for large numbers; hosts love the chance to demonstrate their skill by flaming crêpes at the table.

The first crêpe feature in Volume 9 gave detailed instructions for making crêpes together with some simple recipes, so refer back to it before you start on these more sophisticated dishes.

Basic Crêpe Batter

1½ cups milk
1 cup flour
pinch of salt
1 egg
1 egg yolk
1 tablespoon melted butter
 or oil
little oil (for frying)

6–7 inch crêpe or omelet pan

Makes about 18 crepes (allow 3–4 per person).

Method

Sift flour with salt into a bowl, make a well in the center and add the egg and egg yolk. Pour in half the milk slowly, stirring constantly, then stir in the melted butter or oil. Beat well until smooth.

Add the remaining milk, cover and let stand at room temperature for at least 30 minutes before using. The batter will thicken on standing. It should be the consistency of light cream — if it is too thick, add a little more milk.

Heat the crêpe or omelet pan over moderate heat, add a few drops of oil and turn the pan so it is coated; pour out any excess oil. Add 2–3 tablespoons batter, immediately rolling it around clockwise to coat the base of the pan evenly. Cook over fairly high heat until the crêpe is golden brown on the bottom, then run a thin metal spatula under the edges to loosen the crêpe, raise it slightly with the fingers, slip the spatula underneath and toss or flip the crêpe. Cook about 10 seconds on the other side and turn out onto a paper towel.

Continue making crêpes in the same way, stacking them one on top of the other. Add more oil to the pan only when the crêpes start to stick — they should be cooked in as dry a pan as possible.

If not using crêpes immediately, cover them with a bowl or cloth to keep warm. To store them, place a sheet of wax paper between each one, wrap them in foil or a plastic bag and refrigerate for up to 4 days or freeze them. **Note**: the filled unbaked crêpes also freeze well; thaw them, then bake in a moderate oven (350°F) for 20–25 minutes or until brown.

Toss crêpes or gently flip them with a metal spatula

Quantity Terms

In the following recipes 1½ cup quantity crêpe batter refers to the amount obtained by using 1½ cups milk, with the other ingredients in proportion, not 1½ cups prepared batter (see basic recipe at left).

SAVORY CREPES

Lobster Crêpes

1½ cup quantity basic crêpe batter

For filling
1¼–1½ lb cooked lobster or
 1½ cups (¾ lb) prepared
 lobster meat
3 tablespoons butter
1½ teaspoons paprika
béchamel sauce, made with
 3 tablespoons butter,
 3 tablespoons flour, 1½ cups
 milk (infused with slice of
 onion, 6 peppercorns, blade
 of mace and bay leaf)
1½ teaspoons tomato paste
¼ cup heavy cream
salt and pepper

For sauce
1 cup (¼ lb) finely sliced
 mushrooms
1 tablespoon butter
1 shallot, finely chopped
1 teaspoon onion juice
2 tablespoons brandy or sherry
¾ cup heavy cream
2 tablespoons grated
 Parmesan cheese
 (for sprinkling)

Makes about 18 crepes.

Method

Make the crêpe batter and let stand 30 minutes.

To make filling: if using a whole lobster, split in half lengthwise and discard head sac and intestinal tract running down tail; extract meat from claws, legs and tail and slice it; scoop soft meat from the body. Melt butter in a pan, add the paprika and cook 1 minute over low heat. Add the claw, leg and tail meat (not the soft body meat) or the prepared lobster meat if

For lobster crêpes stir in the cream and paprika-flavored lobster meat to the tomato-flavored béchamel sauce

Spread the crêpes with the lobster filling and fold in three; arrange on an ovenproof platter

using, and cook 1 minute; set aside.

Make béchamel sauce, stir in the tomato paste and the soft body meat, if using a whole lobster, and simmer 2–3 minutes. Stir in the cream and paprika-flavored lobster meat, heat thoroughly and taste for seasoning. Keep warm. Set oven at low (300°F).

Fry crêpes. Put a generous tablespoonful of lobster mixture on each crêpe and fold

For a luxurious entrée, serve a platter of lobster crêpes with a creamy mushroom sauce

them in three. Arrange them, overlapping, in a buttered ovenproof dish and keep warm in the heated oven.

To make sauce: melt butter, add shallot and onion juice and cook until shallot is soft but not brown. Add the mushrooms, increase the heat and cook 1 minute or until moisture has evaporated. Pour in the brandy or sherry and cream, season to taste and boil rapidly for 1 minute. Pour the sauce over the crêpes, sprinkle with cheese and brown under the broiler. Serve at once.

Onion Juice

There are 2 ways to extract onion juice:

1 Cut a slice off the onion and work the onion on a juicer, as you would squeeze a lemon.

2 Cut a slice off the onion. Hold the onion over a piece of wax paper and scrape cut side with a sharp paring knife.

Seafood crêpes — arrange a few shrimps on top before coating with sauce and cheese and browning

Seafood Crêpes

1½ cup quantity basic crêpe
    batter (see page 124)

For filling
1 cup white wine or ½ cup
    clam juice
½ lb flounder fillet
1 cup (½ lb) cooked, peeled
    shrimps
1 cup (½ lb) cooked lobster
    meat or crab meat

For sauce
thick béchamel sauce, made
    with ¼ cup flour, ¼ cup butter,
    2 cups milk (infused with
    slice of onion, 6 peppercorns,
    blade of mace and bay leaf)
½ cup heavy cream
salt and pepper
¼ cup grated Gruyère or
    Parmesan cheese
    (for sprinkling)

Makes about 18 crêpes.

Method
Make crêpe batter and let
stand 30 minutes. Make
béchamel sauce, season well,
cover and set aside. Fry
crêpes.

To make filling: if using
wine, boil it in a pan to
reduce by half. Add flounder
fillet or pour clam juice over
flounder, cover and simmer
gently for 2–3 minutes just
until fish flakes easily. Drain
fish, reserving liquid, and
flake it, discarding bones and
skin. Cut shrimps in chunks
(and the lobster meat if using)
and mix shrimps and lobster
or crab with flounder. Add
1 cup béchamel sauce to bind
mixture and season well.

Put a generous spoonful of
filling on each crêpe, fold in
half; reserve a few shrimps
and arrange on top of the
crêpes before spooning over
sauce, if you like. Arrange the
crêpes in a buttered baking
dish. Set oven at hot (400°F).

To make sauce: add cook-
ing liquid to remaining
béchamel sauce and bring to
a boil, stirring. Add cream,
bring just back to a boil, taste
for seasoning and spoon over
crêpes to coat.

Sprinkle crêpes generously
with cheese and bake in the
heated oven for 12–15
minutes or until the sauce is
bubbling and the top is brown.

Quantity Terms
In the following recipes
1½ cup quantity crêpe
batter refers to the
amount obtained by using
1½ cups milk, with the
other ingredients in pro-
portion, not 1½ cups pre-
pared batter (see basic
recipe, page 124).

Palatschinken

1½ cup quantity basic crêpe
    batter (see page 124)
white sauce, made with
    3 tablespoons butter,
    2 tablespoons flour, 2 cups
    milk
salt and pepper
2 eggs, separated
½ cup grated Gruyère or sharp
    Cheddar cheese

For fillings
choose 3–4 from those on the
    right to give variety

6–7 inch gratin or baking dish

This Czechoslovakian recipe is
an excellent way of using
small quantities of leftover
meat and vegetables. Makes
4–6 servings.

Method
Make the crêpe batter and let
stand 30 minutes.

Fry the crêpes in a pan
slightly smaller than the gratin
or baking dish; prepare
chosen fillings. Grease gratin
or baking dish and set oven at
hot (400°F).

Put alternate layers of crêpe
and various fillings into the
dish, beginning and ending
with a crêpe.

Make the white sauce,
season well, take the pan
from the heat and beat in the
egg yolks, one at a time. Beat
the egg whites until they hold
a stiff peak and fold into the
sauce with 1 tablespoon of
the cheese and season well.

Spoon the sauce over the
crêpes so that it runs down
the sides. Sprinkle the top
thickly with remaining cheese,
and bake in the heated oven
for 20–30 minutes or until
brown and a skewer inserted
in the center for 1 minute is
very hot when withdrawn.

For serving, cut in wedges
like a cake.

Fillings for Palatschinken

Ham: mix ¾–1 cup diced
cooked ham with 2 table-
spoons Dijon-style mustard,
seasoning and 2 tablespoons
chutney.

Lamb: cook 1 sliced onion in
1 tablespoon butter until
brown. Add ¾–1 cup diced
cooked lamb, 2 tablespoons
ketchup, seasoning and 2
tablespoons chili sauce.

Chicken: mix ¾–1 cup diced
cooked chicken with 2
chopped hard-cooked or
scrambled eggs. Season well
and bind with a little chicken
gravy or cream.

Seafood: mix ¾–1 cup diced
cooked, peeled shrimps,
lobster meat or crab meat
with 1 package (3 oz) cream
cheese, softened with 1–2
tablespoons cream. Season
well.

Mushroom: cook 2 finely
chopped shallots or scallions
in 2 tablespoons butter until
soft. Add 2 cups (½ lb) finely
chopped mushrooms and
cook until all the liquid has
evaporated. Stir in 2 teaspoons flour and 5–6 tablespoons stock or milk. Heat
thoroughly, add 2 teaspoons
chopped parsley and season
to taste.

Carrot: heat ¾–1 cup diced
cooked carrots with 2 tablespoons finely chopped onion
in 2 tablespoons butter.
Season and add 1 teaspoon
chopped mint if you like.

Spinach: heat ¾–1 cup
puréed or chopped cooked
spinach in 2 tablespoons
butter or cream; season and
add a little nutmeg.

Cabbage: fry 1 large chopped
onion in 2 tablespoons butter
until soft. Add 6–8 tablespoons cooked chopped cabbage, seasoning, 1 teaspoon
paprika, 2 teaspoons red wine
vinegar and ¼ teaspoon each
of sugar and dill or caraway
seeds.

Tomato: cook 1 finely
chopped shallot or scallion in
1 tablespoon butter until soft.
Add 1 teaspoon tomato paste,
1 teaspoon paprika and 1
tomato, peeled, seeded and
chopped, or ½ cup (4 oz)
canned tomatoes, drained
and crushed. Simmer 2–3
minutes, then add 1 cooked,
sliced country sausage or
frankfurter, and ¼ cup diced
Cheddar cheese. Heat
thoroughly and season.

Cheese crêpes may be made with either Gruyère or sharp Cheddar cheese

Hungarian Crêpes

1½ cup quantity of basic crêpe batter (see page 124)

For filling
1½ lb fresh spinach or
   2 packages frozen chopped spinach
6 tablespoons butter
1 shallot, finely chopped
3 tomatoes, peeled, seeded and chopped
2 teaspoons tomato paste
1 teaspoon paprika
4 hard-cooked eggs, chopped
salt
black pepper, freshly ground

To finish
2 tablespoons melted butter
2 tablespoons grated Parmesan cheese

Makes about 18 crêpes.

Method
Make the crêpe batter and let stand 30 minutes.

To make filling: wash fresh spinach thoroughly and cook in plenty of boiling salted water for 5 minutes, drain and chop. Cook frozen spinach according to package directions and drain well.

Melt 2 tablespoons butter in a pan, add the shallot and cook gently until soft but not brown. Add tomatoes, tomato paste and paprika and simmer 2–3 minutes. Take from the heat, stir in the hard-cooked eggs, season to taste and keep warm.

Fry the crêpes. Heat the spinach in the remaining butter and spread a little on each crêpe. Add a spoonful of egg mixture and roll up the crêpes like cigars. Place them in a heatproof serving dish, sprinkle with melted butter and grated cheese and brown lightly under the broiler. Serve at once.

Gruyère is a valley in the Swiss canton of Fribourg where the original Gruyère cheese was made. A similar cheese, also called Gruyère, is made in the Dauphiné region of France and large quantities of domestic Gruyère are made in this country. True Swiss Gruyère has only a few tiny holes but the French and domestic types have the large holes which are often regarded as characteristic of the cheese. Gruyère is ideal for cooking as it has a dry texture and a rich, nutty flavor, especially when well aged.

Quantity Terms
In the following recipes 1½ cup quantity crêpe batter refers to the amount obtained by using 1½ cups milk, with the other ingredients in proportion, not 1½ cups prepared batter (see basic recipe, page 124).

Gruyère or Cheddar Crêpes

For crêpe batter
¾ cup milk, mixed with ½ cup water
scant 1 cup flour
pinch of salt
2 eggs
2 teaspoons olive oil
2 teaspoons melted butter
½ cup grated Gruyère or sharp Cheddar cheese

For filling
2 cups thick béchamel sauce made with ¼ cup flour, ¼ cup butter, 2 cups milk (infused with slice of onion, 6 peppercorns, blade of mace, bay leaf)
salt and pepper

To finish
1 cup heavy cream
½ cup grated cheese (half Parmesan and half Gruyère, or sharp Cheddar)
1½ tablespoons butter

Diced cooked ham or cooked mushrooms, or grated cheese can be added to the sauce for filling. Makes about 18 crêpes.

Method
Make batter as for basic crêpe batter, adding the oil, butter and cheese after half the liquid has been added. Leave batter to stand 30 minutes.

Make béchamel sauce, season well and keep warm. Set oven at hot (400°F). Fry the crêpes.

Spread a generous tablespoon of sauce on each crêpe and roll them up like cigars. Place them in a buttered ovenproof dish, spoon over the cream and sprinkle with grated cheese. Dot with butter and bake in the heated oven for 7–10 minutes or until brown. Serve very hot.

SWEET CREPES

Cherry Crêpes

1½ cup quantity of basic crêpe batter (see page 124)
1 tablespoon kirsch
sugar (for sprinkling)

For filling
2 cups fresh Bing cherries, pitted, or 1 can (16 oz) pitted dessert cherries, drained
1 tablespoon kirsch

To finish
¾ cup heavy cream
½ teaspoon ground cinnamon
¼ cup chopped almonds, browned

Makes about 18 crêpes.

Method
Make crêpe batter, adding 1 tablespoon kirsch with the egg and egg yolk and let stand 30 minutes.

Pour kirsch over cherries and let stand 30 minutes to macerate.

Set oven at hot (425°F). Fry crêpes. Put 1 tablespoon cherries on each and roll them up like cigars. Put them in a buttered baking dish, sprinkle generously with sugar and bake in heated oven for 4–5 minutes until very hot. Keep warm in a heated oven.

To finish: bring cream to a boil with cinnamon, pour over crêpes and sprinkle almonds on top. Serve at once.

Crêpes Suzette

For crêpe batter
1½ cups milk
1 cup flour
pinch of salt
2 eggs
3 tablespoons melted butter
   or 2 tablespoons oil
1 tablespoon Curaçao, Grand
   Marnier, Triple Sec or other
   orange liqueur

For orange butter
8–10 sugar cubes
2 oranges
6 tablespoons butter
1 tablespoon orange liqueur

To finish
2–3 tablespoons melted butter
   (if reheating)
confectioners' sugar
3–4 tablespoons brandy

Makes about 24 crêpes.

Method

Make batter as for basic crêpe batter, adding the orange liqueur at the same time as the oil or butter. Let stand 30 minutes.

To make orange butter: rub the sugar cubes over the skin of the oranges to remove the zest; the cubes will become saturated with orange oil and the oranges will look quite bald. Crush the sugar, preferably in a mortar and pestle. Cream the butter, beat in the sugar and the orange liqueur and chill. This method of preparing orange butter takes time but it is the best.

Fry crêpes as thinly as possible; because batter is very rich with extra butter or oil and liqueur, it is possible to make them look lacy.

To reheat and serve the crêpes easily at a dinner party: set the oven at low (300°F). Brush a baking sheet with butter, arrange the crêpes, overlapping, on it and brush

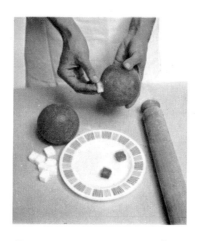

For orange butter for crêpes Suzette, rub sugar cubes over orange rind to remove zest

Add crêpes, orange butter side down, to foaming butter in chafing dish; heat quickly

Turn crêpes, fold in half and in half again; lift onto hot platter. Make sauce and flame

them again with melted butter. Bake them in the heated oven for 5 minutes or until heated through.

Spread each crêpe with orange butter, then fold in half and in half again – this triangular shape is traditional. Arrange crêpes, overlapping, in a warm ovenproof serving dish, sprinkle with confectioners' sugar and keep them warm in the oven while serving the entrée. Just before taking to the table, heat the brandy in a small pan, set it alight and pour over the crêpes.

To Flame Crêpes Suzette in a Chafing Dish

Just before serving dinner, unwrap the prepared crêpes (it doesn't matter if they are cold) and spread each with orange butter. This should be done on the underneath, i.e. the side with spots, because it is not as attractive as the smooth brown side that was fried first.

Stack the crêpes on a plate and put on a tray with a bottle of brandy, a wine glass, metal spatula, fork, tablespoon and 1 tablespoon unsalted butter. Have a chafing dish and a hot serving dish ready.

To serve crêpes: drop the butter in the pan and, when foaming, rotate the pan slightly so the whole surface is lightly coated; put in a crêpe, orange butter side down, heat quickly, turn, fold in half and half again with the metal spatula and fork and lift onto the hot serving platter. Repeat with remaining crêpes. By the time the last few crêpes have been heated, the sauce should be caramelizing on the bottom of the pan – this will give a superb flavor.

Pour 3–4 tablespoons brandy into the wine glass, add it to the pan and shake it so the brandy heats thoroughly. Tilt the pan slightly over the flame so the brandy ignites, and pour the flaming sauce at once over the crêpes. Serve immediately.

Crêpes Suzette, with their traditional orange-flavored sauce, are ready to serve after flaming with brandy

Crêpes Longueville

For crêpe batter
1½ cups milk
1 cup flour
pinch of salt
1 egg
1 egg yolk
grated rind of 1 orange
2 tablespoons sugar
2 tablespoons melted butter
¼ cup blanched almonds, finely chopped

For filling
6 Golden Delicious apples, pared, cored and thickly sliced
grated rind and juice of ½ lemon and ½ orange
¼ cup apricot jam
pinch of ground cinnamon
½ cup heavy cream, stiffly whipped

To finish
1 tablespoon melted butter
2 tablespoons confectioners' sugar

Makes about 18 crêpes.

Method
Make batter as for basic crêpe batter, adding the grated orange rind with the eggs and the sugar with the melted butter. Cover and let stand 30 minutes. Do not add the almonds until just before frying the crêpes.

To make filling: put apples in a pan with lemon and orange rind and juice and the apricot jam. Cover and cook gently for 10–15 minutes or until thick and pulpy.

Add the almonds to the crêpes, fry them and stack on a warm plate. Stir the cinnamon into the whipped cream and fold into the apple mixture. Spread a little over each crêpe. Fold them in four and place, overlapping, in a buttered ovenproof dish. Set

oven at hot (425°F).

To finish: brush with the melted butter, sprinkle with confectioners' sugar and bake in the heated oven for 5–8 minutes or until glazed and shiny.

Crêpes Creole
(with Macaroons and Kirsch)

For crêpe batter
1 cup milk
¾ cup flour
pinch of salt
1 egg
1 egg, separated
1 tablespoon melted butter or olive oil
1 large macaroon, crushed
2 tablespoons kirsch

For filling
1 small fresh pineapple, diced, or 1 can (14 oz) pineapple chunks, drained and diced
¼ cup sweetened pineapple juice (from can if using canned pineapple)
sugar (optional)
6 tablespoons apricot jam
¼ cup kirsch

To finish
2 tablespoons melted butter
confectioners' sugar

Makes about 12 crêpes.

Method
Make batter as for basic crêpe batter, reserving 1 egg white. Let stand 30 minutes.

Just before frying crêpes, beat egg white until it holds a stiff peak and fold into crêpe batter with macaroon crumbs and kirsch.

To make filling: mix pineapple with pineapple juice, sugar to taste if needed, and heat quickly in a pan. Stir in the apricot jam and 1–2 tablespoons kirsch.

Set oven at hot (425°F). Fry crêpes.

Put a spoonful of pineapple mixture on each crêpe, fold in three and arrange, overlapping, in a buttered ovenproof dish.

Brush crêpes with melted butter, sprinkle with confectioners' sugar and bake in heated oven for 4–5 minutes until very hot. To serve, pour remaining kirsch over the hot dish, flame it and serve at once.

To Peel and Cut Fresh Pineapple
Slice off bottom of pineapple with a serrated-edge knife. Hold pineapple firmly and with a sharp stainless steel knife cut down between 'eyes' at a 45° angle. These should come out easily in strips (see photograph). Remove the plume, slice flesh thinly and cut out core with an apple corer. This method disposes of the 'eyes' but avoids waste.

Crêpes à la Crème

1½ cup quantity basic crêpe batter (see page 124)

For pastry cream
2 egg yolks
¼ cup sugar
1½ tablespoons flour
1 tablespoon cornstarch
1½ cups milk
piece of vanilla bean, or strip of lemon or orange rind
1 egg white

To finish
confectioners' sugar
¼ cup slivered almonds

3–4 metal skewers

Makes about 18 crêpes.

Method
Make the crêpe batter and let stand 30 minutes.

To prepare pastry cream: beat egg yolks with half the sugar until mixture is thick and light. Add flour and cornstarch with a little of the milk and mix until smooth. Heat remaining milk with vanilla bean or orange or lemon rind and stir into egg yolk mixture. Return mixture to pan and bring to a boil, stirring constantly.

Watchpoint: it is very important to heat this mixture gently or the eggs may curdle before the flour is cooked.

Simmer pastry cream 1–2 minutes, stirring. Remove vanilla bean or orange or lemon rind. Beat the egg white until it holds a stiff peak, then beat in the remaining sugar until the mixture is glossy. Fold this into the hot pastry cream, and keep warm in a water bath.

Fry the crêpes, spread each one with pastry cream, fold them in three and arrange on a hot buttered dish.

To finish: sprinkle thickly with confectioners' sugar and mark in a lattice pattern with skewers that have been heated under the broiler or in a flame until red hot – it is easiest to heat several skewers at once. Sprinkle with the slivered almonds and serve very hot.

mixture, spoon over the crêpes and serve.

Quantity Terms
In the crêpe recipes $1\frac{1}{2}$ cup quantity crêpe batter refers to the amount obtained by using $1\frac{1}{2}$ cups milk, with the other ingredients in proportion, not $1\frac{1}{2}$ cups prepared batter (see basic recipe, page 124).

Crêpes aux Framboises
(Raspberry Crêpes)

$1\frac{1}{2}$ cup quantity of basic crepe
    batter (see page 124)
1 tablespoon kirsch
confectioners' sugar (for
    sprinkling)

For filling
2 packages frozen raspberries,
    thawed
2 teaspoons arrowroot
2 tablespoons sugar, or to taste
1 tablespoon kirsch

Method
Make the crêpe batter, adding 1 tablespoon kirsch with the egg and egg yolk, and let stand 30 minutes.

Drain the raspberries and reserve them. Mix the arrowroot to a paste with 2 tablespoons of the raspberry juice and bring the remaining juice to a boil. Stir in the arrowroot paste until the juice thickens, take from the heat and stir in the kirsch with sugar to taste. Let cool and stir in the raspberries.

Set oven at hot (400°F) and fry the crêpes.

Put a tablespoon of raspberry mixture on each crêpe, roll the crêpes up like cigars and arrange them on a heatproof platter. Sprinkle with a little confectioners' sugar and bake in the heated oven for 4–5 minutes or until very hot. Heat the remaining raspberry

Crêpes can be layered with filling on an ovenproof platter

MEASURING & MEASUREMENTS

The recipe quantities in the Course are measured in standard level teaspoons, tablespoons and cups and their equivalents are shown below. Any liquid pints and quarts also refer to U.S. standard measures.

When measuring dry ingredients, fill the cup or spoon to overflowing without packing down and level the top with a knife. All the dry ingredients, including flour, should be measured before sifting, although sifting may be called for later in the instructions.

Butter and margarine usually come in measured sticks (1 stick equals $\frac{1}{2}$ cup) and other bulk fats can be measured by displacement. For $\frac{1}{3}$ cup fat, fill the measuring cup $\frac{2}{3}$ full of water. Add fat until the water reaches the 1 cup mark. Drain the cup of water and the fat remaining equals $\frac{1}{3}$ cup.

For liquids, fill the measure to the brim, or to the calibration line.

Often quantities of seasonings cannot be stated exactly, for ingredients vary in the amount they require. The instructions 'add to taste' are literal, for it is impossible to achieve just the right balance of flavors in many dishes without tasting them.

Liquid measure	Volume equivalent
3 teaspoons	1 tablespoon
2 tablespoons	1 fluid oz
4 tablespoons	$\frac{1}{4}$ cup
16 tablespoons	1 cup or 8 fluid oz
2 cups	1 pint
2 pints	1 quart
4 quarts	1 gallon

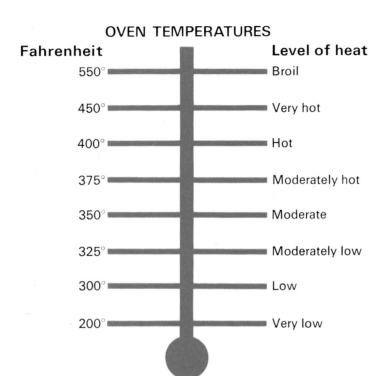

OVEN TEMPERATURES

Fahrenheit		Level of heat
550°		Broil
450°		Very hot
400°		Hot
375°		Moderately hot
350°		Moderate
325°		Moderately low
300°		Low
200°		Very low

OVEN TEMPERATURES AND SHELF POSITIONS

Throughout the Cooking Course, oven temperatures are stated in degrees Fahrenheit and in generally agreed levels of heat such as 'high' and 'moderate'. The equivalents are shown on the table above.

However, exact temperature varies in different parts of an oven and the thermostat reading refers to the heat in the middle. As the oven temperature at top and bottom can vary as much as 25°F from this setting, the positioning of shelves is very important. In general, heat rises, so the hottest part of the oven is at the top, but consult the manufacturer's handbook about your individual model.

Pans and dishes of food should be placed parallel with burners or elements to avoid scorched edges.

When baking cakes, there must be room for the heat to circulate in the oven around baking sheets and cake pans; otherwise the underside of the cakes will burn. If baking more than one cake in an oven that has back burners or elements, arrange the cakes side by side. If the oven has side burners, arrange cakes back and front.

Oven thermostats are often inaccurate and are unreliable at extremely high or low temperatures. If you do a great deal of baking or question the accuracy of your oven, use a separate oven thermometer as a check on the thermostat.

(Volume 13)

Acknowledgments
Photographs on page 8 by Fred J. Maroon; on page 83 by Robert Goodyear; on page 88 by Alan Spain. Other photographs by Michael Leale, John Ledger, John Cowderoy, Gina Harris and Roger Phillips.

NOTES